D1034268

MOSTLY
WHAT
GOD DOES

MOSTLY

WHAT

GOD DOES

Reflections on Seeking and
Finding His Love Everywhere

SAVANNAH
GUTHRIE

W Publishing Group

An Imprint of Thomas Nelson

Mostly What God Does

© 2024 Savannah Guthrie

All rights reserved. No portion of this book may be reproduced, stored in a retrieval system, or transmitted in any form or by any means—electronic, mechanical, photocopy, recording, scanning, or other—except for brief quotations in critical reviews or articles, without the prior written permission of the publisher.

Published in Nashville, Tennessee, by W Publishing, an imprint of Thomas Nelson.

Thomas Nelson titles may be purchased in bulk for educational, business, fundraising, or sales promotional use. For information, please email SpecialMarkets@ThomasNelson.com.

Unless otherwise noted, Scripture quotations are taken from the Holy Bible, New International Version®, NIV®. Copyright © 1973, 1978, 1984, 2011 by Biblica, Inc.® Used by permission of Zondervan. All rights reserved worldwide. www.zondervan.com. The "NIV" and "New International Version" are trademarks registered in the United States Patent and Trademark Office by Biblica, Inc.®

Scripture quotations marked ESV are taken from the ESV® Bible (The Holy Bible, English Standard Version®). Copyright © 2001 by Crossway, a publishing ministry of Good News Publishers. Used by permission. All rights reserved.

Scripture quotations marked KJV are taken from the King James Version. Public domain.

Scripture quotations marked MSG are taken from THE MESSAGE. Copyright © 1993, 2002, 2018 by Eugene H. Peterson. Used by permission of NavPress. All rights reserved. Represented by Tyndale House Publishers, a Division of Tyndale House Ministries.

Scripture quotations marked NAB are taken from the New American Bible, revised edition. Copyright © 2010, 1991, 1986, 1970 Confraternity of Christian Doctrine, Washington, DC, and are used by permission of the copyright owner. All rights reserved. No part of the New American Bible may be reproduced in any form without permission in writing from the copyright owner.

Scripture quotations marked NASB are taken from the New American Standard Bible® (NASB). Copyright © 1960, 1962, 1963, 1968, 1971, 1972, 1973, 1975, 1977, 1995, 2020 by The Lockman Foundation. Used by permission. www.Lockman.org

Scripture quotations marked NCB are taken from the New Catholic Bible, Copyright © 2019 by Catholic Book Publishing Corp. All rights reserved.

Scripture quotations marked NIRV are taken from the Holy Bible, New International Reader's Version®, NIrV®. Copyright © 1995, 1996, 1998, 2014 by Biblica, Inc.® Used by permission of Zondervan. All rights reserved worldwide. www.zondervan.com. The "NIrV" and "New International Reader's Version" are trademarks registered in the United States Patent and Trademark Office by Biblica, Inc.®

Scripture quotations marked NKJV are taken from the New King James Version®. Copyright © 1982 by Thomas Nelson. Used by permission. All rights reserved.

Scripture quotations marked NLT are taken from the Holy Bible, New Living Translation. Copyright © 1996, 2004, 2015 by Tyndale House Foundation. Used by permission of Tyndale House Ministries, Carol Stream, Illinois 60188. All rights reserved.

Any internet addresses, phone numbers, or company or product information printed in this book are offered as a resource and are not intended in any way to be or to imply an endorsement by Thomas Nelson, nor does Thomas Nelson vouch for the existence, content, or services of these sites, phone numbers, companies, or products beyond the life of this book.

Names and identifying characteristics of some individuals have been changed to preserve their privacy.

ISBN 978-1-4003-4112-2 (HC)
ISBN 978-1-4003-4114-6 (eBook)

Library of Congress Control Number: 2023948593

Printed in the United States of America

24 25 26 27 28 LBC 8 7 6 5 4

For Vale and Charley

CONTENTS

PART 4: GRACE

PART 5: HOPE

PART 6: PURPOSE

FOREWORD

orward. That's a good word. That's how it strikes me to be writing a book, well, about anything, let alone faith. It is a bit . . . forward. A bit bold, a bit audacious, a bit terrifying, a lot bit intimidating.

This isn't even how you do it. "Forewords are written at the beginning of a book by someone else," my editor informs me gently—and deletes it.

Dah! You don't write your own foreword! Not if you know what you're doing!

Well. Onward.

In Washington, DC, where I lived and worked as a reporter for many years, you might hear an old joke, an amusing line, toward the end of a long congressional hearing or at one of those "grip and grin" political dinners marked by airplane chicken and bottomless glasses of too-sweet chard. The afternoon is drawing long and the energy droops, or the long day is fading into a longer evening, way past bedtime in a city that *wants* to sleep. And yet, one by one, they keep going, speaker after speaker, speech after uninspired speech. In the nation's capital, if you get a turn at the dais or the podium, you do not pass it up. You do not take one millisecond less than the time allotted, no matter how restless or borderline hostile the audience may grow.

That's when you might hear it. The poor soul slated last to talk ambles up to the mic and with feigned self-awareness chuckles, "Well, everything's been said, but not everyone has said it." Big laughs. Big, big, desperate laughs—then on to the prepared remarks, abbreviated none whatsoever.

That line returns to me as I set out on this project. Everything has been said about faith, but I have not said it. What, then, can I possibly add? What can I say that has not already been expressed better—more fluidly, more profoundly, more originally, more convincingly? What qualifications or expertise do I have? I am no religious scholar or historian, I speak no ancient language, I did not attend seminary (unless you count vacation Bible school?). I have no special proficiency.

At church, my pastor always apologizes when he tells the congregation a personal story or life anecdote that he knows they've heard from him before. "I'm sorry!" he says sheepishly. "I only have this one life!" In a way, I feel the same. I have just this one life, and it is certainly not an example to hold up for others or a monument to great righteousness or faith. It's just a life of a person who has felt the love of God and been saved by it, over and over and over again.

I like to tell people about the God I know. The one whose hand rests gently on my shoulder, whose presence I can feel behind and beside me when I'm under pressure. The one whose persistent but kind nudging can prod me into perspective, whose forbearance and tenderness can coax me into change. The one who surprises and delights me with the imagination of his creation and the beautiful potential of his humanity. The one whose revelations spark my intellect and ignite my passions and purpose. The one who melts me with unexpected favor and unmerited generosity. The one who holds me, firmly and purposefully, when the weight of my disappointments and setbacks threatens to crush.

I like to tell people about that God I know. To tell that story—well, like the politician at the rubber-chicken dinner, I am not going to pass up my moment at the mic.

When I started to think about this book, a phrase from my childhood strangely and persistently popped into my head: *Six Easy Pieces*—it was a memory from piano lessons, a yellowing old pamphlet of sheet music with six classics, stored in the piano bench amid the piles of books and paper. It was such a gauzy recollection, I wasn't confident I was even remembering it correctly, that such a thing ever really existed. *Six Easy Pieces*—I just liked the way it sounded. Accessible and intriguing at the same time.

I like to tell people about the God I know.

An internet search confirmed the piano book memory. But then, I Alice-d my way down the Google rabbit hole and discovered something else: a famous book titled *Six Easy Pieces: Essentials of Physics Explained by Its Most Brilliant Teacher.*[1]

Oh, you don't know it? The essentials of physics explained by its most brilliant teacher? Perhaps, like me, you've fallen behind on your science manuals!

It got me thinking. What are the essentials of faith? If faith could be broken down into six easy pieces, what would those building blocks be? What are the six foundational aspects of a connection to God? Here is what I came up with:

Love.

Presence.

Praise.

Grace.

Hope.

Purpose.

These six not-so-easy pieces are my road map for this project: a collection of reflections and a sort of spiritual manual. I've never done this before, and I am right beside you as we go. This is for us! You may be faith-full, you may be faith-curious, you may be faith-less, still scarred by a toxic religiosity of your past. You may have thought you were buying a raconteur's rip-roaring memoir of adventures in journalism and law (sorry!). Whatever may be, come as you are.

———

Every night when I put my kids down, we have a ritual. It's the usual bath, brush, book, (bicker), bed routine. Right before lights out, my husband or I lie down next to them. We say our prayers. And then we say, "Thirty seconds . . . starting now."

Thirty seconds of silence. We just lie together. In the best-case scenario, the kids drift off to sleep, and I gingerly tiptoe out of the room. More commonly, they start jabbering ("Mom, what's the plan for tomorrow?"), and I have to restart the thirty seconds all over again.

But the routine is meant to provide quiet and simple togetherness. Thirty seconds of space. That's what I'm imagining for us at the end of each essay as we go on this journey together.

In my vision, this book will be by your bed, read in the morning with your coffee or, perhaps, right before you turn in at night. And . . . it is meant to be not read. After every essay, you'll find a blank page. It isn't necessarily meant to be written on (though you can, of course). The page is empty to remind us to sit with whatever thoughts have risen within us.

Blank space. Quiet. Nothingness. This is where God has the greatest opportunity to do his thing.

(In case you're wondering, connecting with us is his thing.)

I'm also imagining this book would be read slowly. Not all at once. An essay here and there. I'm envisioning you read a chapter, let some time pass, think about it, read another. You don't even have to start at the beginning. Start at the end; skip around. Start at the middle and double back to the beginning. There is no correct order. Heck, you could drop it on the floor, pick it up wherever the book opens up to, and just start reading. I don't mean to micromanage. This is your book, you bought it (thank you!); you do you. I just have a feeling that it will be most meaningful if it is stretched out slowly over time.

Enough preamble. Thank you for picking up this book and trusting me. I'm bringing nothing but my curiosity and a receptive heart. I'm open to what God might be saying to me and might want me to share with you. I'm ready to be surprised and delighted.

God will not let us down.

Forward.

PART 1

LOVE

CHAPTER 1

ALL MY LOVE

When I was fifty-one, I got my first tattoo. I never thought I'd get a tattoo; I certainly didn't think of myself as a tattoo person, whatever that means. And more to the point, for most of my life, I didn't feel strongly enough about anything to mark my body permanently with it. Even after I had kids—certainly the deepest and most timeless human love I can imagine—I never considered tattooing their initials on my arm or ankle or back (or neck) (or face). I am the kind of person who one-clicks something from Amazon and then frantically moves to cancel it before the sale goes through.

But here I am, typing with a hand whose arm now bears a tattoo.

Three simple words: *All My Love*. It is an exact copy of my father's handwriting, traced from a love letter he wrote my mother when they were courting six decades ago. My mom discovered the letter when my son was born. I was determined to name him after my father, who died suddenly when I was sixteen years old. My father's name was Charles, but everyone called him Charley. Or was it Charlie? For the life of me, I couldn't remember how the nickname was spelled. I could still see his signature written on checks or bills, but what I remembered was formal: *Charles E. Guthrie* or sometimes *Chas. E. Guthrie*. He never signed those things with a nickname.

So the spelling was a matter of hot debate in my family—and important—because I planned for my second child, a boy, to go by the nickname. With the due date deadline ticking, my mom produced the evidence, unearthing a letter from some box tucked deep away in the closet that somehow, miraculously, didn't get raided by us as kids or tossed out by her in a huffy cleaning spree. She didn't share the letter's contents with me, but when my son was born, she had the signature superimposed on a photo of my father, and there it was: *All My Love, Charley*.

All my love. It is a link to my father and a personal mantra to glance down and live up to—a mindset for daily life. But most importantly, it is an encapsulation of what all my years have taught me about faith. All my love: imagine the words spoken by our heavenly Father; to me, it is the simplest, most direct description of his ambition for our world and his intentions toward us.

It may seem like a throwaway, a shallow slogan no better than a bumper sticker or comment on Instagram—or worse, a breezy sign-off when trying to get off the phone ("gotta go love ya bye"). All I know is it took me a long time, a lifetime of church and no church, faith and not much faith, seeking and failing, hoping and falling, to understand this basic precept: mostly what God does is love us.

I first ran across those words in a version of the Bible called *The Message*. A scholar named Eugene Peterson—rather audaciously—decided to translate the entire Bible, not just into English but into . . . well, plain English. Not exactly slang, but not exactly *not* slang. Something grounded, easy to grasp, and earthy. The old King James Version of the Bible, with its *thees* and *thous*, and even modern translations can sometimes seem remote and out of reach. But Peterson thought about how Jesus spoke—not in a posh or educated dialect but the common, conversational, street language of his time. Peterson paraphrased the entire Bible this way. The result is fascinating, provocative, sometimes beautiful and brilliant, and sometimes disappointing. I have turned to it many times over the years, as a way to jump-start a reflection or see a scripture in a new way.

That was how I came across a reimagined version of these famous verses from Ephesians:

Follow God's example, therefore, as dearly loved children, and walk in the way of love, just as Christ loved us and gave himself up for us as a fragrant offering and sacrifice to God.

Ephesians 5:1–2

Fine and lovely, vaguely encouraging, yet somehow distant and removed. This is how you might have heard it in church or seen it in Bible study. But what I read that day in *The Message* was a thunderbolt.

> Watch what God does, and then you do it, like children who learn proper behavior from their parents. Mostly what God does is love you.
>
> Ephesians 5:1–2

The simplicity of the words and the unadorned plainness of their truth were a revelation.

Where is God and what is he up to? Mostly what God does is love you.

How does God feel about me? Mostly what God does is love you.

What job should I take? Where should I live? Whom should I marry? Do I forgive that person? Do I deserve forgiveness? Am I shallow? Am I selfish? Am I unworthy of love? Have I broken my life? What does God think about the choices I've made? Mostly what God does is love you.

These simple words amounted to a radical reframing of my concept of God. They grabbed me and held my heart.

It is so easy to conflate the critiques of our parents, our culture, or our own harsh self-judgments and subconsciously attribute them to God—especially when we are distant from his presence. "God" can take on the persona of a nebulous, looming, always-angry father figure whom we imagine must be sitting in scornful judgment, waiting to deliver our just comeuppance.

Mostly what God does is love us.

Or when life is cruel, when loss comes, when disappointments mount, when the world we inhabit seems to be a monument to injustice and unfairness and arbitrariness—it is hard to

It is so easy to conflate the
critiques of our parents,
our culture, or our own
harsh self-judgments and
subconsciously attribute them
to God—especially when we
are distant from his presence.

———————————————————————

believe that God is doing anything, let alone loving us specifically and meaningfully.

Mostly what God does is love you. To believe this about God is the essence of faith: giving God the benefit of the doubt in a world that invites cynicism and despair. I've always felt believing in God isn't really the hard part; believing he is good and actively engaged in our lives and the world in the face of so much pain—that is the hard part.

God does not require us to ignore or gloss over the sorrows we experience or the unjustness we see but to believe past them. Believe that he is on the case, that his intentions toward us are good, that he is ever inclined toward forgiveness and reconciliation. That the pains of this world are not his original plan and will not be how the story ends. This is faith.

I've had a relationship with God since I was a little girl; I cannot remember a time when he was not a presence in my consciousness. My early childhood was a churchy one, with Sunday school and choir practice and even Wednesday night (!) services. One of my earliest memories is seeing my mother, father, and teenage brother in white robes at the front of the church as the pastor baptized them in a giant Jacuzzi-looking tub. There were five of us Guthries: my parents, my two older siblings, and me. But my sister used to say that God was the sixth member of our family.

I have always believed in God. But I have not always found it easy to believe that he is unfailingly good, or at least well-intentioned toward me. There have been seasons I have been disappointed with him, icing him out, or too ashamed to face him. When I say *seasons* I don't mean weeks or months, but years. Years of just kind of "keeping in touch" here and there with my faith, not much tending to my relationship with God. These times used to make me feel guilty and nervous, like I was living on the edge and outside his will, not doing the things I should, not even praying, let alone any other spiritual practice.

I have also had times of deep devotion. For a few years in my late twenties and early thirties, I went through a time of enthusiastic Bible study, devouring scriptures, keeping little notebooks of favorite verses, and memorizing them. It was a fruitful time. Then I stopped. For years. For reasons I can't exactly pinpoint. A combination of busyness and distraction, and, yes, disappointment and disenchantment with God over the things in life that weren't going my way. So I checked out.

These verses stayed in my mind, however. They popped up at opportune moments, unexpectedly, in a way that felt divine, like a lifeline God threw out, reconnecting me to him. I was grateful for it but sheepish. Embarrassed that God was still hanging in there with so little to work with, guilty that I hadn't cracked my Bible to learn anything new in years. *I'm really coasting on fumes*, I would think to myself. I held that shame for a long time.

But I don't think of it that way anymore. Here's the "mostly what God does is love you" way of looking at these circumstances. In a season of close connection, God shored me up with wisdom and his Word; he provisioned me for a long journey, even one that I would at times choose to walk alone. Instead of feeling guilt for not keeping up with devout practices, imagining that God was disappointed or disgusted

To believe this about God is the essence of faith: giving God the benefit of the doubt in a world that invites cynicism and despair.

with me or had written me off entirely, what if I believed that what he was really doing was loving me the whole time?

It is powerful when we look at the events of our lives in this light. Mostly what God does is love you.

This is not "God-light," or a feel-good ideology with a dash of the divine mixed in. This is the hardest stuff. But if we can truly believe it, it is transformative. Love like that takes root and is a revolution from within. A triumph over hopelessness. A way to reimagine and rethink every circumstance, even those that disappoint us. Especially those.

Imagine it—God loving you. Seeing you, appreciating you, delighting in you. Knowing you, having compassion on you, healing you, forgiving you. See it, appreciate it, grasp it, hold on to it. Inhale deeply of his goodwill and attune yourself to evidence of his love. Look for it everywhere.

What you will find is that love like that is not just for you. It is for the world. For love like that cannot be contained—it is exuded and exhaled outward.

> Watch what God does, and then you do it, like children who learn proper behavior from their parents. Mostly what God does is love you.
>
> Keep company with him and learn a life of love.
>
> Observe how Christ loved us. His love was not cautious but extravagant. He didn't love in order to get something from us but to give everything of himself to us. Love like that.
>
> Ephesians 5:1–2 MSG

Love like that.

This is our great commission: choose to believe in God's love. Wrap yourself in it; let it warm you from the inside. Then go out into the world, and you do it too.

CHAPTER 2

BLINKING CURSORS

Disclaimer.

You know those pharmaceutical advertisements that are always on—the ones for futuristic-sounding drugs to cure niche illnesses nobody's ever heard of? "Imchafin" relieves chronic scratchy wrists. Try "OoflaXYZ" for wasp-bite-related dry eye. Five seconds of advertising, twenty-five seconds of gauzy images of Elderly Couple Holding Hands or Middle-Aged Woman on Pilates Reformer as the voice-over unfurls a laundry list of ghastly-sounding side effects:

"Trixcedrin" may cause drowsiness, insomnia, loss of appetite, loss of hearing, loss of sight, loss of car keys, excitability, irritability, hyperactivity, depression, gout, bunions, or vertigo. Call your doctor or scream into the abyss if these, or any other side effects, occur.

At some point, you wonder why they bother.

Anyway, this is my disclaimer section. Cue scene of me serenely riding a bicycle along a picturesque mountain path.

This is not a memoir. I have never wanted to write a memoir. Not in a conventional sense. For one thing, it seems like a lot of work. For another, I don't remember all that much from my career. I've even joked that if I ever wrote a personal or professional history, it would be called *What Happened?*—with a question mark, not a period. Not *What Happened.* But . . . *What Happened?* Like, no, really, what *did* happen? I'm sure, with a little effort or hypnosis, I could call up a few funny old war stories or news capers from back in the day, but honestly, what's the point? My stories could never be as interesting as Diane's or Katie's or Oprah's. And anyway, it was mostly a blur. A good blur, but still a blur. Wake up, cover story, do live shot, cover story, do live shot, do live shot, do live shot, sleep, rinse, repeat.

When I told my friend Jenna Bush Hager that I was writing a book about faith, she was highly encouraging. Jenna is an inveterate reader and an accomplished author herself. I confessed to her that I was worried I wouldn't have enough to say, not enough material to fill a whole book. "Sure, you do!" she encouraged. "Like that time a couple months ago when you were sick with a fever and sweating in bed with hot flashes and you woke up in the middle of the night and had that big epiphany about God! You could write about things like that!"

"What are you talking about?" I replied. No memory. Nothing. Zero. Not only do I not remember the contents of the "epiphany" I apparently had in my fever dream (and neither did she, by the way), I don't even remember having the epiphany in the first place.

I can't write about what I can't remember.

And I can't write about other things—things I do remember but I don't want to talk about. For instance, I don't want to write about getting divorced. It was one of the hardest, saddest times of my life. It almost broke me. I got married when I was thirty-three and was so idealistic and hopeful for some perfect family picture. In retrospect, I was a little delusional and a little stubborn. I wanted to not be single anymore, to have a family. I wanted the fairy tale. I always had miserable luck in the romance department. Bad choices, lack of self-esteem—bleh, it's really not an original story. I ran out of patience because I thought I was running out of time. I got married when I shouldn't have.

I'm not getting into it, like I told you, but that marriage did not work out. There is no scandal here, just disappointment. There are other things I want to write about even less, things that happened when I was much younger, bad-luck kinda things that were a great source of shame and embarrassment for many years. I'm not getting into the details, and don't drive yourself wild imagining the absolute worst. I'm just mentioning it because, in a book about faith, you have to talk about your struggles. Going through deep crises, profound adversity—those are the make-or-break moments for faith; they can be existential threats to your belief, or they can be extraordinary teachers. Sometimes they are both, and not always at the same time.

Going through deep crises, profound adversity—those are the make-or-break moments for faith; they can be existential threats to your belief, or they can be extraordinary teachers.

I write about those kinds of feelings here. You might wonder what I could be alluding to. You might even wonder if I've really faced any adversity at all. What business do I have to weigh in on these topics? What are my suffering credentials? That's fair, and this is a book about connecting to God; a relationship with him doesn't happen in a vacuum. It happens in real life, with real circumstances and events and human interactions. I've heard it said life can sometimes feel like you're walking barefoot with God on a burning-hot sidewalk. I'm just saying that I don't want to delve into why the sidewalk was hot, how it got that way, what its temperature was, how badly my feet were scalded. I just want to tell you how God carried me and healed me and what I learned from the experience.

Okay? Okay.

CHAPTER 3

THE BONUS COMMANDMENT

D o you remember the old *SNL* character Stuart Smalley? (If not, highly recommend a Google!) Clad in a fuzzy sweater with a mop top of blond hair, he was a bundle of insecurity who gave himself cringe-inducing pep talks in the mirror: "I'm good enough, I'm smart enough, and doggone it, people like me!"[1] It was simultaneously funny and painful to watch. Funny because it was painful.

For me, the skit was always uncomfortable for another reason.

I had (and maybe still have?) a visceral aversion to any expression of self-love and self-regard. Growing up, the whole personal affirmation thing was a big no-no at home and at church. We were raised not to brag, not to get "too big for your britches," and, above all, to be humble. I still remember hearing a sermon on this subject when I was about nine or ten years old. Actually, it wasn't even a sermon; it was an anecdote at the beginning of a sermon, one of those amusing stories preachers tell to break the ice or illustrate a point. If only this pastor knew his impact on the little girl sitting in the audience. He told the tale of the time he had prayed to the Lord for humility—a prayer that coincided with a ski excursion at the top of a snowy peak just as he was poised to take a run. Moments after his devout prayer, he tripped, fell, and careened down the ice in a big, painful, embarrassing display. The story got a big laugh in the auditorium. Be careful what you pray for—ha ha ha ha! But I was not laughing. This harmless little yarn ended up having a profound, lifelong impact on me. The lesson I took away: remain humble, or God will humiliate you.

Humiliation, to me, was a great peril, one of the worst things that could happen to a person. I think this was unique to my psyche; to this day, I am the kind of person who is easily embarrassed. Even something silly, like someone telling me I have lipstick on my teeth—I'm glad they told me, sure, but secretly horrified, wishing I could briefly evaporate from the scene. I have an early memory of feeling totally humiliated by my father in front of some grown-ups. They sat around a table one afternoon, chatting, as I breezed by, unconsciously pulling my undies out of my rear end (aka fixing a wedgie).

"Are you going to the movies?" my father asked as his pals chuckled.

"Huh? No, why?" I asked him.

"Because you're picking your seat."

Dumb, corny, no-harm-intended dad humor. And yet I will never forget how ashamed and stupid I felt at that moment. My dad probably shouldn't have made a joke at the expense of a fragile tween. But on the other hand, I was a highly sensitive kid. For me, the micro-mortifications were everywhere.

So I was vigilant about maintaining humility, lest I suffer my greatest fear: humiliation. The movement toward self-love and self-acceptance was full speed ahead in our culture, but I was not on that train. It all seemed self-indulgent and slightly sinful, and God have mercy if you slipped and started getting prideful or thinking too highly of yourself. Then it would be you reeling down that ski slope in a blaze of un-glory.

"Love your neighbor as yourself" (Mark 12:31). It's one of the earliest Bible verses I remember being taught. It is, of course, a Sunday school classic—a way to convince unruly five-year-olds not to slug each other (with a mild infusion of religious pressure). It also pairs nicely with that old kindergarten party line, the Golden Rule: do unto others as you would wish them to do unto you.

Even as a child, I grappled with the last part of the verse. "Love your neighbor" was an easy enough concept to grasp (not so easy to do but easy to understand). But "as yourself"? I found the notion perplexing. I thought God could have used a better example, maybe a commandment like, "Love your neighbor as you love ice cream." Because I didn't "love myself" that way at all. In fact, I was pretty sure doing so was wrong.

Still, I made peace with the old "love your neighbor" verse. I decided that God was really saying something different. He was essentially saying to care about your neighbor as much as you care about yourself. Think about your neighbor as much as you think about yourself. If we can all agree on anything, it's that humans constantly think about themselves. So the commandment was basically this: turn your self-obsession outward and apply some of that preoccupation to others.

This interpretation satisfied me for many years—until recently when I listened to an audio meditation on an app called Hallow. I was gifted a subscription when Mark Wahlberg, a contributor to the app, came on *TODAY* to promote it. Always a sucker for a freebie, I began using it on my morning commute.

I chose a daily meditation called *Lectio Divina*[2], an ancient method of reflecting on a section of Scripture. There are many versions of the practice, but basically, it involves the repeated reading of the same verse, listening each time for different aspects of the text with long spaces of silence in between. On the first reading, you just listen, allowing the words to wash over you. On the next reading, you listen, attuned to whichever particular word or phrase jumps out at you. On a third reading, you might listen and imagine yourself in the scene as it is described. Again, and most importantly, in between each reading, silence. This is where the magic happens, where the Spirit just might move you.

This was the daily verse I came upon on Hallow early one morning while driving to work in the dark:

[He asked,] "Of all the commandments, which is the most important?"

"The most important one," answered Jesus, "is this: . . . 'Love the Lord your God with all your heart and with all your soul and with all your mind and with all your strength.' The second is this: 'Love your neighbor as yourself.' There is no commandment greater than these."

Mark 12:28–31

Oh, this old saw again, I thought. I returned to my favored adaptation: love yourself is not literal. It just means we should pay as much attention to others as we do ourselves. But then a thought occurred, the kind of revelation that feels otherworldly and buzzes with electricity. In a way, a bonus commandment was hidden within the two that Jesus mentioned. Love the Lord God. Love your neighbor. And love yourself.

I've come full circle. I believe God truly intends us to love ourselves. Humiliation, shame, self-berating, and browbeating are not God's intention for us. But neither is self-aggrandizement or puffery. I don't know about you, but I can't generate genuine feelings of self-love by whispering affirmations to myself. It feels phony and occasionally pathetic—à la Stuart Smalley. The proper balance is struck with the secret ingredient: God himself. Knowledge of and belief in the deep love of God is how we come to love ourselves.

Yes, humility is a positive spiritual attribute. But humility is not humiliation; it is not being forcefully brought down low—either by ourselves or by God. Humility is simply recognizing our need for

In a way, a bonus
commandment was
hidden within the two
that Jesus mentioned.
Love the Lord God.
Love your neighbor.
And love yourself.

God. Acknowledging our need, as opposed to telling ourselves we're fully self-sufficient, leaves space for him. That space can and will be filled with his love for us. This love

Humility is simply recognizing our need for God.

is how we begin to love ourselves—we see ourselves as God sees us. It is the foundation of a real, unshakable confidence.

God loves us, and his love is contagious. If we stick close to him, we can't help but catch it.

CHAPTER 4

LIKE A MOTHER

I was forty-two years old when I gave birth to my first child. I didn't wait that long to have kids because I was too busy being a "career girl," or because I was galivanting around the bars single and fancy-free, or because I was unsure about parenthood. If I had my choice, I probably would've gotten married in my twenties, had three kids, and never left my hometown.

Sometimes life doesn't work out the way we wish it would. To which, at some point, we all will likely say a resounding "thank God." Thank God I didn't take that job. Thank God I didn't make that move. Thank God we didn't get that house. Thank God I didn't marry that person I was absolutely, totally, certainly sure was the only one for me—in high school.

That said, I always knew I wanted to be a mom. Frankly, I assumed I would be. I never anticipated how hard it would be to find a life partner. My twenties and thirties were a tour de force of bad romantic decisions. I watched all my friends pair off and lilt down the aisle, wondering if it would ever be me. The years went by; the bridesmaid dresses piled up. Somehow, I was always lucky in my career and unlucky in my personal life. In my midthirties, I finally got married but it was short-lived (see previous disclaimer— not discussing it!), and after I found myself divorced at thirty-six, I was pretty sure I was damaged goods, past my prime in every way, especially reproductively.

God had better plans.

I met my future husband, Michael Feldman, at his fortieth birthday party. I wasn't invited, but I wasn't exactly a party crasher. My friend, who was dating Mike's friend, invited me to come along. I was covering the 2008 presidential campaign, slogging from town to town, out on the road for months except for brief overnights at home to switch out the clothes in my suitcase. One of those campaign furloughs fell on a Saturday night, and my friend Ann insisted I get out and do something "fun." That's how I found myself at a party full of people recognizable from politics and media, but to me total strangers. I knew not one soul. Ever the gentleman, Mike walked up and introduced himself to the new girl in a red dress. He was wearing a dark blue suit with a pale blue pocket square. He joked that his seventy-five-year-old father had dressed him. (I still have the red dress; I dragged it out a decade later to surprise him at his fiftieth birthday party.)

For Mike and me, it was like at first sight. We both were commitment-phobes for different reasons (he was a forty-year-old

Sometimes life doesn't
work out the way we
wish it would. To which,
at some point, we all will
likely say a resounding
"thank God."

_____

bachelor, after all!). But we immediately bonded; we had an inherent, instinctive respect and trust and affection for each other. We proceeded to date for—wait for it—five and a half years. Talk about waiting for it! We hemmed and hawed, dillied and dallied, talked the relationship to death while frittering away precious time—much to the chagrin of our families and friends ("Why don't you guys just get off the dime and commit! Or break up! Enough already!").

God had better plans.

In May 2013, at the sprightly ages of forty-five and forty-one, we got engaged, setting our wedding for March in my hometown of Tucson, Arizona. We had talked about kids many times and were eyes wide open that it wouldn't be easy. We assumed we'd be going the fertility treatment route, likely a long haul with no guarantees. But by great fortune (and, I believe, divine blessing), I got pregnant, and in August 2014, our daughter was born.

I will never forget laying eyes on Vale for the very first time. I can still see the doctor lifting up her little frame high in the air to give me the first glimpse. "It's a girl!" he exclaimed. "She's a chunker!" She was eight pounds, nine ounces of sheer miracle. I felt a combination of ecstasy and shock—how could it be that what was nothing nine months before had turned into such a profound something? I cradled her face to mine. Cheek to cheek, my girl and I. The tears tumbled out, a dam-like release from a place deep within, as though lying dormant until precisely this moment. I knew these strange and lovely tears were always, only, meant just for her. Two years later, weeks shy of my forty-fifth birthday, my little firecracker Charley wailed his way into the world. Our family was complete.

My kids are simultaneously my greatest joy and my most

searing daily challenge. Loving them has made my life meaningful. Because I came to parenthood later in life, long after I had given up hope, I do not take it for granted. When Charley was six weeks old, I brought both kids home to Tucson to visit my mom. My cousin Teri, who was like an aunt to me growing up, drove down from Phoenix to see us. "Oh, Savannah," she said, her eyes glistening as she watched me with my babies. "It's all you ever really wanted."

Motherhood. What a revelation. Physically. Emotionally. Intellectually. And yes, spiritually. I can think of no other experience that has more enhanced my understanding of God.

To me, parenthood is God's ultimate real-life metaphor; it is the closest humans will ever get to grasping how God relates to us. It is no accident the Scriptures refer to him as our heavenly Father, and us, his children—the nearest approximation of God's love for us is parent to child.

In my experience, God's revelations are always much more about show-and-tell than scrolls and edicts from the mountaintop (except for Moses that one time). Being a mom has been quite the show-and-tell for me, bringing home, in the most profound and personal way imaginable, what God must be thinking and feeling at any given moment.

It's worth taking a moment just to ponder it. How we feel about our kids is how God feels about us. The way we adore them. The way they make our hearts leap with joy. The way we revel

To me, parenthood is God's ultimate real-life metaphor; it is the closest humans will ever get to grasping how God relates to us.

in their personalities and gifts and quirks. The way we glory at their milestones and accomplishments, no matter how minor. Watching them grow is like witnessing the unfolding of a flower in real time, a gift we get to open and reopen every day.

God's connection to his children is stunningly intimate and tender—like a mother to her child. I don't know about you, but I can scarcely take that in. It is overwhelming to imagine that God could feel that way about me. Too good to be true. But transformative if truly absorbed.

God's great metaphor does not end there. Every parent knows that to have children is to carry a joyous burden of worry and fear and concern. The famous quote is famous for a reason: "To have a child is momentous. It is to decide to have your heart go walking around outside your body."[1] When my cousin had her first baby, I asked her what it was like. She said, "It's like having a thorn. You love that thorn, but it is a thorn."

Our kids worry us. Challenge us. And they frustrate us, sometimes to our breaking point, especially when we are just trying to ward off disaster, only looking after their best interests. From explaining to a toddler why they can't have ice cream for breakfast to telling a tween why she isn't allowed on social media, it is often an exercise in exasperation and helplessness.

If only I could make them do what is good for them! How I wish I could just make them understand that the things I'm doing or forbidding—it's for their own good! It is not to be cruel or withhold happiness from them. I'm on their side!

Now imagine those words from God. About us. And we begin to grasp his perspective toward his children.

We are imperfect humans who stumble and fail. We make bad decisions. Things go wrong and we don't understand what God is doing. We complain and rebel. We withdraw, sulk, and give God the silent treatment. We can't see the big picture. Like kids who are incapable of seeing the long view ("One day you'll thank me I didn't let you get a face tattoo!"), we don't have a wide enough perspective. We are only human. We don't have the multidimensional vantage point of God, taking account of people, places, and events, of future and current and past.

But like a good parent, God does not let this get to him. He does not grow impatient. He does not rage. His love, compassion, and unwavering commitment never fail—regardless of how we act, what we say, or what we "deserve." And his forgiveness is always available when, inevitably, we fall. When we turn to him, we find him waiting with outstretched arms.

My son, Charley, had a protracted "mean to mommy" phase when he was four. Like so many toddler phases, it lasted much longer than I could tolerate. "How was your playdate today, sweetie?" I remember asking him once. "I had such a good time. I forgot about you," he replied. "And I wanted to forget about you." (Yes, I wrote down the exact quote.) I worried I was raising a little boy who hated me. I even called the pediatrician, who laughed and said, "Oh, they're meanest to the ones they feel the closest to!"

Toddlers are like little scientists, watching everything and gathering data: *What happens if I throw this? What happens if I press there?* In this case, the "there" he was pressing on firmly was my heart. Intellectually, I could understand that he was just testing,

God does not grow
impatient. He does not
rage. His love, compassion,
and unwavering
commitment never fail.

taking his personality out for a spin. I attempted to keep a stoic face in front of him, maintaining a cool exterior—then, I would close the door and cry actual tears because a little boy hurt my feelings. Let's face it: kids often are their worst at home. They walk in, kick off their shoes, dump out their backpacks all over the floor and their emotional baggage all over Mom.

But here's the thing that parenthood has taught me—something unique to any other kind of relationship. It does not matter how our kids act; our love for them is unshakable.

So it is with God.

This is the bedrock truth that motherhood has brought home to me in the most visceral way.

God's feelings for us have nothing to do with our feelings toward him.

His thoughts toward us have nothing to do with our thoughts toward him.

We cannot do or say anything to make him love us more—or less.

He loves us not because of who we are or what we do but because of who he is and what he does.

He loves. Like a mother. But better.

The LORD your God in your midst,
The Mighty One, will save;
He will rejoice over you with gladness,
He will quiet you with His love,
He will rejoice over you with singing.

Zephaniah 3:17 NKJV

CHAPTER 5

YOU'RE SOAKING IN IT

When my daughter, Vale, was about two years old, we were listening to a CD of hymns that my mom had given us. Yes, we still had a CD player in 2016. Don't tell me there aren't miracles! My mom had sent me an album of church music not long after the baby was born, and her intent was not subtle: let's make sure this little girl has some God in her life.

I can't say sleep schedules, potty training, and attaining pacifier sobriety didn't take precedence over spiritual development in the early years, but at some point in her toddlerhood, I rediscovered the old CDs and decided to give them a spin. Notwithstanding my mom's concern, I had been taking Vale to church so she wasn't a total pagan. That's how it came to pass that, one day, while we were listening to the music and busying ourselves doing whatever we used to do then—blocks? Barbies?—when "Jesus Loves Me" came on, her little blue eyes lit up. "That's my song!" she exclaimed.

Jesus loves me, this I know.

That's my song too. And yours.

There have been moments in my life when I have been overcome by a sense of being loved by God. A warmth, an ecstasy even—a feeling that is so sweet and unmistakable I am certain that the Spirit of God is with me. It can come unexpectedly, triggered by a song, a sunset, or a verse that suddenly comes to mind. It can also come upon me for no reason at all. But I know it is him. I recognize him, the way you can sense when someone familiar walks into the room. I smile at him in my mind. *There you are. I see you. Thank you.* It is an exquisite feeling.

Now remain in my love.

John 15:9

"Remain in my love." It's Jesus' urging, recorded by the apostle John. Versions of this sentiment are all through the Scriptures, so you know he really meant it. It's a good thought. It always reminds me of that old Palmolive commercial from the 1970s. Madge the manicurist is tsk-tsking as she tends to the dry, mottled hands of her young client. "It's from dishwashing," the attractive young housewife bashfully explains. Madge is ready with the answer: "Try Palmolive—softens your hands while you do dishes!" she says.

Cut to the housewife's hands resting in a dish of green liquid. "You're soaking in it!"

The housewife jerks her hands away in horror; Madge gently presses her fingers back into the little dish. Finally, the housewife relents, letting go to luxuriate in the green goo.

God's love. Are you soaking in it? I'm not. Not most days.

The only thing harder than believing that "mostly what God does is love you" is maintaining that belief. Holding on to a feeling of being cherished, special, and adored feels not only difficult but even self-indulgent in the face of the chaos of the world. Walk down the street or through the grocery store or turn on the news and you'll be confronted with people experiencing heartache and struggle, in disaster and in need. In this life, the pain is real. Who are we to walk around basking in the feeling of being the blessed of God? It feels tone-deaf, selfish, borderline offensive.

Less globally, more personally: feeling loved when confronting setbacks and disappointment and loss is damn near (can we curse in a book about faith?) impossible. It's all well and good to feel loved by God when things go your way. When you struggle—with need or conflict or hurt—forget it. Forget about feeling loved by God; these are the moments we feel opposed by God. We feel abandoned by him.

And equally as challenging, perhaps, are all the in-between moments, the monotonous days in and days out—ordinary, repeated twenty-four-hour units of to-dos and to-don'ts, go heres and go theres stacked up one after the other, from day to week to month to year. Sure, God loves us, but honestly, who has time to sit around soaking in it? We have dishes to do, meals to plan (translation: order from Grubhub), playdates to arrange, jobs to hold down, memos to write, Zooms to withstand, bosses to satisfy or placate or dazzle. We have spouses and partners to pay attention to, children not to ruin, family and friendships to nurture or enjoy or overcome. It's a full-time business, this life stuff.

How do we summon and maintain that feeling of being loved? It's pretty simple. We don't. Because it's not a feeling; it's a fact. To "remain in God's love" is a frame of mind. We use our brains to remind our hearts. We may not be able to sustain the emotion of being loved by God, but we can remain in the knowledge of being loved by God. We can remain in the memory of being loved by God—and let that sow confidence within us that nothing about his posture toward us has changed.

It reminds me of marriage in a way. Anyone who's been in a relationship for a while knows that you don't stay in love forever like some starry-eyed teenager (sorry, sweetie!). Marriage is an act of will and volition: deciding that you love that person, and that person loves you—every day. A relationship with God is just that—a relationship.

Scripture speaks of us being "rooted and established in love" (Ephesians 3:17). The plant metaphor is apt. I once heard a pastor in New York City named Timothy Keller speak of marital relationships in these very terms. He said that marriage is like a garden. And if you've ever had a garden, you know how much work it takes. You have to be in it every single day. If it's dry outside, you have to water. But if it rains, you still have to get in there, pruning and weeding. You have to work in that garden every day—and still, it takes years before it starts looking any good.

To "remain in God's love" is
a frame of mind. We use our
brains to remind our hearts.

Our relationship with God can sometimes feel like that. If we can choose to root ourselves in love, making it our home base, everything else blossoms from that foundation.

> And I pray that you, being rooted and established in love, may have power, together with all the Lord's holy people, to grasp how wide and long and high and deep is the love of Christ, and to know this love that surpasses knowledge— that you may be filled to the measure of all the fullness of God.
>
> Ephesians 3:17–19

It is a choice every day to remain in God's love, actively believing it, looking for it everywhere, choosing to interpret circumstances in that light. It amounts to giving God the benefit of the doubt, attributing good intentions to him. Even in times of hardship, asking yourself, *How is God loving me in this moment?* Willing yourself to search for the evidence of his love, remembering that God said, "You will seek me and find me" (Jeremiah 29:13).

Whatever we encounter—a difficult person, a disturbing event, a confounding scripture—if our surface reaction or immediate takeaway is inconsistent with the unassailable fact of God loving us, then we must keep looking. We must go deeper. Because his loving us is a certainty.

If our surface reaction is inconsistent with God loving us, we must go deeper. Because his loving us is a certainty.

Perhaps you've heard of the apostle John, one of Jesus' twelve disciples. He authored one of the four gospels and several other books in the New Testament. There's something curious and notable in his writings. In recounting the life of Jesus, he repeatedly referred to a particular disciple as "the one whom Jesus loved."

> So she came running to Simon Peter and the other disciple, the one Jesus loved, and said, "They have taken the Lord out of the tomb, and we don't know where they have put him!"
>
> John 20:2

> Then the disciple whom Jesus loved said to Peter, "It is the Lord!"
>
> John 21:7

> Peter turned and saw that the disciple whom Jesus loved was following them.
>
> John 21:20

I could go on. Over the years, scholars and theologians have largely agreed on the identity of this disciple. So who was the mystery person John described as "the one whom Jesus loved"? John. He was talking about himself. Of course.

When I first learned this, I was slightly amused. How highly must he have thought of himself, I marveled, that he would pay himself this (repeated) compliment! Overconfident much? But then I was moved.

This is the embodiment of what it means to "remain in my love." John was not bragging; this was not a flex. Nor was he claiming and hoarding this love all to himself; he didn't say he was the only one Jesus loved. He just matter-of-factly conveyed what he considered to be his most significant feature.

John Piper, a pastor and Christian author, said, "Perhaps this is John's way of saying, 'My most important identity is not my name but my being loved by Jesus the Son of God.' He's not trying to rob anybody else of this privilege; he is simply exulting in it: 'I'm loved, I'm loved, I'm loved—that's who I am. I'm loved by Jesus.'"[1]

It's a child hearing "Jesus Loves Me" and saying, "That's my song." It's an apostle witnessing the Messiah and saying, "I'm the one he loves." But it's a fact that belongs to all of us.

This is all deeply personal, of course. I don't know the steps that will work best for you to "remain in his love" on any given day. But I know everything would change for us if we could. Who would we be if we really believed this?

> No power on earth or in hell can conquer
> the Spirit of God living within the human
> spirit; it creates an inner invincibility.[2]
> **Oswald Chambers,**
> *My Utmost for His Highest*

Love Triangle

"As the Father has loved me, so have I loved you. Now remain in my love. If you keep my commands, you will remain in my love, just as I have kept my Father's commands and remain in his love."

John 15:9–10

"This is my command: Love each other."

John 15:17

And:

"The most important [commandment]," answered Jesus, "is this: . . . 'Love the Lord your God with all your heart and with all your soul and with all your mind and with all your strength.' The second is this: 'Love your neighbor as yourself.' There is no commandment greater than these."

Mark 12:29–31

In diagram form:

Remain in God's Love

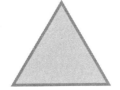

Love God   Love Each Other

PART 2

PRESENCE

CHAPTER 6

PRESENT TENSE

Where is God? What is his exact location?
He is now.
He is not in a place; he is in a moment.
This one.
Every one.
Eternally.

———

> God said to Moses, "I AM WHO I AM. This is what you are to
> say to the Israelites: 'I AM has sent me to you.'"
>
> Exodus 3:14

All the way at the beginning, there it is, right there—in the
very name God used to announce himself to Moses.

I AM.

Present tense.

God is here. Now.

Pause.

Stay awhile.

Be present.

God is always communicating here in the present tense.

———

I once heard a pastor say God is like a radio station that is always
on, always transmitting. Whether we tune in is up to us. Whether
we turn up the volume or leave it as background noise—again, our
choice.

God is here, now, and his speaking to us does not depend on
our speaking to him. His thoughts about us do not depend on our
thoughts about him. He doesn't wait to come until he is called. We
don't summon him with our pious practices and diligent spiritual
routines. They help us tune in. They open the window through
which his light is ready to shine. But he is present to us, whether or
not we are present to him.

God is here, now, and
his speaking to us
does not depend on
our speaking to him.

Come near to God and he will come near to you.

James 4:8

You can remember him from the past and find confidence.
You can imagine him in the future and find hope.
But in the now, that's where you find him.

CHAPTER 7

GOD'S TELEPHONE NUMBER

A long time ago, when I first moved to New York City, I found it difficult to find a church that I connected with. Mostly, I didn't try all that hard. (A boozy brunch can be much easier to find on a Sunday morning than the perfect spiritual home.) But other times, I church-hopped around town, the proximity to my apartment being my main criterion. It was on one such occasion that I visited an old, historic-looking church—the kind that you know was once magnificent but had long fallen into neglect. It was different from the kind of churches that usually appealed to me; this one was traditional and liturgical. *Almost mechanical*, I remember thinking. Sweet but stodgy. The hymns were slow and dreary, the organ loud and plodding. *Ugh*, I thought, wondering how long the service was, certain it would be "one and done" for me at this particular house of worship. (Yes, those thoughts were interspersed with self-scolding for expecting a church to entertain or dazzle me.)

Then the older, robed, priest-like figure ascended to the dais to deliver his sermon. He had a warm and kind demeanor but wasn't exactly C. S. Lewis in the pulpit. His message seemed to amount to "Have a nice day." I started to fade. But his enthusiasm was disarming, and he caught my attention when he asked the congregation a surprising and quirky question.

"Do you know God's telephone number?"

Blank stares and silence were returned from the sparsely occupied pews. "Well, do you?" he asked with a boisterous chortle. "It's Jeremiah 33:3!"

> "Call to me and I will answer you and tell you great and unsearchable things you do not know."
>
> Jeremiah 33:3

The first thing I learned that day at the boring old church: there is no wasted time spent with God. You can always get something out of it if your heart is in the right place. (Or, as in my case, even when it's not.)

And the second thing: God's telephone number. Just call. He will answer you.

Let's agree on something. Prayer is hard, for countless reasons. We are busy. We are distracted. We are tired. We aren't sure it's working. Sometimes we are sure it's not.

I'm not good at praying. I may start out okay, but before you know it, my meandering mind roams off topic, and my prayers devolve into worry sessions or to-do lists. What begins as praying turns into internally organizing playdates or pickups.

That's hard enough. Sometimes it is our emotional mindset that makes prayer feel intimidating or impossible. When we are angry, wounded, or bitter, sometimes it is all we can do to even consider praying. Other times, our concerns and

Let's agree on something. Prayer is hard, for countless reasons.

fears are so overwhelming that we don't even know where to begin. The famous scripture from Romans meets us right where we are:

> We don't know what we should pray for. But the Spirit himself prays for us. He prays through groans too deep for words.
>
> Romans 8:26 NIRV

As usual, I love the wording from *The Message*:

He does our praying in and for us, making prayer out of
our wordless sighs, our aching groans.

Romans 8:26

He doesn't even need words from us. Just a sigh, a tear, or a whimper. He knows. What an amazing resource we have in a God who already understands our whole history, our intricate emotional fabric, our every inner thought. We don't have to explain anything. It's like having a Super Therapist—or as the Bible puts it, a "Wonderful Counselor" (Isaiah 9:6).

I am so grateful that God can take what I bring—my mixed motives, misery, and miscellaneous mishigas—and fashion it into prayer. In a way, prayer, at its essence, is simply processing our feelings and emotions and concerns in the presence of God. It is our intentional turning to him.

In our moments of weakness, in our moments of deep need and helplessness, sometimes the best we can do is just to come. Don't worry. He can work with that.

> He doesn't even need words from us. Just a sigh, a tear, or a whimper. He knows.

Maybe you've heard that famous quote: "80 percent of success in life is just showing up."[1] In prayer, it's 100 percent. By simply arriving to a quiet moment with God, its purpose is accomplished.

This doesn't mean your prayer is instantly answered or that

In a way, prayer, at
its essence, is simply
processing our feelings and
emotions and concerns in
the presence of God. It is our
intentional turning to him.

you reopen your eyes and feel better or different. Prayer is a success simply if you do it. Because whether you perceive it right then and there or not, you are building something together with God. You are building a connection—the fact of it, if not the immediate feeling. It may be much later before you realize the depth of the foundation that has been formed.

This we know: God meets us in prayer. He said so, definitively: "Call to me and I will answer you." It is a bedrock promise.

You place the call. Yours is one he will always pick up.

CHAPTER 8

HE SPEAKS OUR LANGUAGE

"The gatekeeper opens the gate for him,
and the sheep listen to his voice.
He calls his own sheep by name and leads them
out. When he has brought out all his own,
he goes on ahead of them, and his sheep
follow him because they know his voice.
But they will never follow a stranger; in fact,
they will run away from him because they
do not recognize a stranger's voice."

John 10:3–5

How do we hear and recognize God's voice? It's one of the most important and challenging aspects of faith. Here, the Bible returns to one of its favorite metaphors. God is the Shepherd; we are his sheep.

Tangent alert: Have you ever wondered why humans couldn't have been a more impressive animal in these allegories? Perhaps a magnificent bird? Or how about a cheetah? Sheep aren't exactly majestic. And they have a terrible reputation. For being dumb. Or blind. Or always getting lost. Or frightened by just about everything.

On the other hand, in this passage, the sheep are having a moment. They're discerning—they know their caretaker's voice and follow him. And they're shrewd—they're not fooled by an impostor. They spot the counterfeit a mile away and wisely skedaddle.

Sheep—they're just like us?

Maybe on our good days. It is incredibly hard to hear God's voice in our whirring, mile-a-minute culture of commotion. The internet is loud. The news is loud. Our music is loud. Our kids are loud. Our problems are loud. Our distractions are loud.

And God is described as having "a still small voice" (1 Kings 19:12 NKJV). No wonder we miss so much.

When I had my first baby, I was amazed at something. Well, a lot of things: her little squeaks, her sweet sighs, her pretty rosebud lips. The astonishing, *adult truck driver* volume of her burps. But back to the subject. Somehow, even though she was only days old, she seemed to recognize my voice.

Newborns are fascinating, but let's face it, they don't do much. Some say the first month of life is really the tenth month of gestation; infants aren't ready for the world but are just too darn big for the womb. (When I was pregnant with Charley—who came into the world early at nearly ten pounds—I was so enormous that my work colleagues said my belly entered the room thirty seconds before I did.)

In those first weeks, newborns mostly sleep and cry and barely open their eyes. And even when they do, they can't see much. But babies can hear—and much more than just the indistinct clang and clamor of the world. By the time they are born, many newborns know and recognize the sound of their parents' voices. In Vale's first few weeks, sometimes I swear I could see it happen: this tiny lump of flesh, barely days old, eyelids shut tight, reacting—stirring, shifting, eyes flickering—when my familiar voice entered the room.

Let's underline the point. How could my little newborn seem to recognize her mother's voice from the moment she entered the world? Because we had spent a lot of time together. We had been intimately connected. Inseparable—literally. She would know my voice anywhere.

And so it is with our relationship with God. If we want to recognize God's voice, an intimate connection is vital. Moments spent together, just logging time. We must do life with him, like a baby does with Mom.

We can extend the metaphor even more (yay, let's!). Think about someone you really know. Your spouse, your sibling, your parent. Not only do you recognize their voice but you also know their tone. You know their inflections. You know what they're saying— even if they don't come right out and say it. For example, when I

If we want to recognize God's voice, an intimate connection is vital. Moments spent together, just logging time. We must do life with him.

ask my husband, "Would you want to put the kids down tonight?" I am really saying, "You should put the kids down tonight." I am not really asking. He knows me so well that he knows what I mean.

(Luckily, God is not passive-aggressive.)

To be quiet enough to hear God's voice, we need more than a quiet place; we need quiet in our spirits and our souls. We need to make space for him, just being present to him—hearts open, ears peeled.

And by the way, quietness is hard. Stillness is hard. This is not a prerequisite, yet another impossible threshold we have to cross before God will speak. But it sure makes it easier to hear him when he does.

———

Over the years, I feel I have experienced God's voice maybe a time or two at most. And it wasn't a booming, loudspeaker, *Voice of God* voice of God. It was an assertive, surprising, and quasi-intruding thought that seemed to emanate from somewhere outside of me.

Kristin Chenoweth, the Broadway actress, once told me that for her God's voice feels like a "handprint" on her heart, an impression she feels deep within.[1] I like how she said that.

You might wonder: How do you know the voice you hear is not just your own internal dialogue? Or worse, your own self-soothing or wishful thinking?

I don't have a perfect fail-safe to guard against that. But in my experience, when I hear God's voice, it is usually saying something I never expected to hear him say. It is foreign to me, consistent with who God is, echoes the Bible, and doesn't always tell me what I want to hear.

A few years ago, in my midthirties, I was going through a difficult time in my personal life. Day after day, I prayed. I wrote in my journal, sought refuge in the Scriptures, beseeched God for an answer. The prayers varied depending on the particular heartache du jour, but they amounted to the same request: save me, deliver me, help me, rescue me. I prayed this prayer day after day, week after week, months into years. Nothing seemed to change. Then, one day, I received a surprising response. A thought crashed into my consciousness like a comet, so jarring and unexpected it stopped me in my tracks.

I am rescuing you.

I knew this thought did not come from within myself, because it was the last thing I felt or believed. I didn't feel rescued in that moment. Quite the contrary. I felt abandoned and alone. Yet someone—God?—seemed to be telling me that he was, in fact, in the midst of rescuing me.

I can't say this thought comforted me in the moment—not exactly. But it was impossible to ignore. Its authority and unexpectedness forced me to consider it. What if God is, in fact, rescuing me? Right now? At this moment? In the middle of my misery? In the hard times, when nothing seems to be improving?

The sentence stuck with me. In the near term, I found some comfort in what God seemed to be communicating to me. If nothing else, he was saying, *I'm here. I haven't forgotten you.* Later, with the benefit of years and distance and perspective, I understood it more fully. In that moment, when God said, *I am rescuing you,* he was saying something like this:

This, Savannah. This is the rescue.

This moment, this pain, this anguish—this is the path to freedom. This is the road that will lead you out. Because this is what will force change.

This is how I am rescuing you.

(Spoiler alert: he did rescue me.)

"The gatekeeper opens the gate for him, and the sheep listen to his voice. He calls his own sheep by name and leads them out."

John 10:3

Back to the sheep.

I love this part of the scripture. He calls us by name. It means more than just he knows who we are. He knows how to reach us. Our God knows exactly what speaks to us.

These days, we hear a lot about "love languages." In marriage, especially, we might learn that our partner receives love in a different way than we do. My love language might be Mike putting down the kids for me. Mike's love language might be . . . a foot massage (please, God, no).

God knows our love language. Think about the times you felt touched by him. It could be through a person, an interaction, a song, or a scene in a movie. God knows what moves us. He knows how to connect to our hearts. And words don't constrict him. Sometimes he doesn't need words at all.

Years ago, someone I know told me the most beautiful and astounding story about how she came to faith.

Her name was Susan. She had spent her twenties as a grad student. She decided to live for a year in Ireland. She found a little town in a distant part of the country and moved there to do her studies. She explained to me that the type of academic research she was doing called for her to live and work and move among the people, to become part of their community. One day a bunch of schoolchildren burst into her kitchen, walking right through the door, and asked her bluntly why she never went to church. "You must be a terrible sinner," they told her in their sweet Irish lilt.

God knows exactly what speaks to us.

A while back, I wrote to her and asked her to tell me the story again. She wrote right back.[2]

Well, long long ago, far far away, I was a graduate student in anthropology, travelling the world and learning about other cultures through immersion. I lived in various places and ultimately settled on Ireland as the place about which I wanted to write my dissertation. So I lived in a remote fishing village and learned to speak the language, Gaelic.

I had a manual typewriter and I would have my experiences, and then sit in the kitchen of the big old empty farmhouse I let, which overlooked a craggy cliff with crashing sea below, next to a coal stove, and write my field notes. One day a gaggle of children pushed into the kitchen (doors are never locked, and knocking is unnecessary). I looked at them expectantly, not a clue why they were there. A young girl was pressed forward to speak for the group and said, "Sure Mum says you must be an awful sinner." I was shocked and asked "Why?" She said, "Sure you never go to church." "Huh?" says I. "Sure you never step foot in the church," says she.

I realized I was not doing a very good job of blending in. One of the key tenets of anthropological research is to truly become part of whom and what you are studying. So I knew I had to show up at the village church tucked up the top of the boreen, and blend in.

Not easy for a Jewish girl raised to avert eyes when looking at a cross, ("He is not OUR savior" . . . "G-d does not take human form" etc.). Not easy when it is a tiny church and you don't know the first thing about attending a church service—and doubly hard when you don't understand a bit of what is said, because the mass is in Gaelic. The Gaelic I was learning was colloquial, what was needed to order a pint in the pub or shop at the grocer. My Gaelic was earnest and heartfelt but extremely limited.

So into the mass I sat, squished into a tight pew with the women. The church was the simplest church I had ever seen. I had been in the grand cathedrals—London, Paris, New York, Rome . . . but as a tourist. This tiny church was a one room building, like a one room schoolhouse, white-washed walls, wooden pews, one small window up high behind the altar through which streamed golden light. And a plain wooden cross, no frightening-looking dead Jesus draped across it. I could bear to look at it. I wanted to look. The simplicity of the church, the pure loveliness of the light, the feeling of being one with the people I was learning to know as the postman, the schoolmaster, the farmer, melted me. We were all the one, one heart beating together, as one. The feeling of being united for a greater good opened my eyes and opened my heart. I sat and I listened not understanding a single word. But I loved the sound. . . .

As the mass went on, I felt a peace in my heart and a silence in my soul the likes of which I had never felt. It was as if God was warming his hands right inside me, and I could feel him. I could hear him. I could feel the peace of Christ that passes all human understanding, though I did not have language for it then. But felt it I did.

My friend Susan did not come to belief right away. In fact, her path toward faith was an agonizing, yearslong journey. But it began there, in that tiny Irish church.

I have never forgotten this story—a young woman, of a completely different religion, who met God sitting in a simple church hearing a Mass in words she literally could not understand. But God speaks our language.

In fact, in the particular language of every human heart, he is fluent.

So what is God's voice saying to you? Well, that's between you and him, isn't it?

But to return to the metaphor Jesus loved, it is actually quite clear. The shepherd calls the sheep. In its simplest form, God is always calling. He knows our name.

If we really listen, we will know his voice. And always, boiled down to its very essence, he is saying one thing: "Come with me."

CHAPTER 9

SPOONING
WITH GOD

I'm doing that meditation on the app again. *Lectio Divina*. The narrator reads a portion of Scripture three times, interspersed with long periods of silence. After the final reading, the voice directs the listener: "Now, let go of any effort, and just rest with God."

I try. I really do.

Rest, rest, rest. This is me, resting. I am resting with God.

I need to hurry up and rest and get on with my day.

Rest, already!

The mind wanders, like a baby crawling off a mat.

I attempt to create a visual. What would it be like to rest with God? How to imagine resting with God? It's a struggle. Even in my mind, I can't find a comfortable spot. I try lying down on a blanket on a grassy field, facing up, looking at the blue sky above. I place God next to me, facing up too. Maybe he is holding my hand?

No. Scratch that. I am sitting upright, in a chair, but a comfy one that reclines, or maybe it's a couch, and he is sitting next to me. We are shoulder to shoulder, arms at our sides, our pinkies touching. I sit with it for a minute. Me and God. It feels awkward. Like a bad first date. It doesn't feel relaxing or comforting.

Rest with God; just rest with God.
I am not resting.
When my daughter can't sleep, she makes sure no one else can. She barges into my room, just as my own eyes are growing heavy. "Mom, I can't fall asleep. Help me! What should I think about?"
Bleh, how should I know? I grumble to myself. "Think about horses or carousels or rainbows," I tell her. "Think about horses on carousels made of rainbows. I don't know how to tell you to rest, honey. Just go to bed."

Now I am her. *God, what should I think about?*
I fidget, I stir.
Why is rest so hard?

Another day. Attempting the visual again. Maybe I'm lying down on my bed, on my side, knees tucked in, arms bent, hands folded in prayer under my head. This is how I like to sleep. Fetal position. Now I'm comfortable—much better. Snuggled in tight, blankets wrapped around me all the way to my shoulders. But where to put God in this scenario? I don't like anyone to cuddle up next to me. Discard. I don't want to spoon with God.

Even the thought of closeness makes me fidget.

Just rest with God.

It's the day after Easter. Today's verse has to do with Jesus' pierced hands—the scarred limbs he offered as proof to skeptical disciples. Flashback. I used to imagine holding God's hand when I was a little girl. When I was afraid or needed comfort, I closed my eyes and visualized my tiny fingers wrapped up in his warm, gentle, solid hands.

Suddenly, out of nowhere, a different image invades my consciousness. I am remembering my father's hands. His palms, specifically. They were so smooth. I had forgotten how flat and soft and smooth they were—almost lineless? No lines, no fortune. He did die young, I suppose. I haven't thought about my dad's palms in a long time.

Be still, my heart.

Rest.

I can't place God next to me, even in my imagination.
Because there is no place that can contain him.

> The heavens declare the glory of God; the
> skies proclaim the work of his hands.
>
> Psalm 19:1

God is in the breeze, God is in the air. God is next to me, invisible and everywhere.

God is in my inhale and my exhale.

God is in my ears, in my hearing and listening.

I imagine him as a musical sound, a single note rising just above the din, lingering sweetly, with no beginning and no end.

Breathing.
  Listening.
    Tingly hands.
      Discomfort.
        Letting go.
          Being.
            Here he is.

Just be here now, and let God do the rest.

Let *God* do the rest.

Let God *do* the rest.

Suddenly, I see.

CHAPTER 10

PRAYING WHEN YOU CAN'T

E very night when Mike and I tuck our kids into bed, our prayers are part of the ritual. Usually, it's man-to-man coverage; he takes one, and I take the other. We swap out at halftime, passing each other in the Jack and Jill bathroom they share, high-fiving as we trade kids to close out the day. (Kidding about the high fives!)

Our prayers are heartfelt but at this point a bit rote.

Dear God, thank you for this day, thank you for Mommy, Daddy, Vale, and Charley—our family. Thank you for [rotating assortment of extended relatives]. Dear Lord, help Vale/Charley to remember they are loved and protected, surrounded by your angels, treasured and adored. Help us be the best we can be, remembering to share all we have. Now bring your peace and calm over Vale/Charley; may they rest in the knowledge that God loves them and Mommy and Daddy love them too. Amen.

I'd like to tell you that our sublime children listen carefully and thoughtfully, heads bowed in deep reverence. It's more like nonstop interjections with spiritual concerns such as: "Do I have gymnastics tomorrow?" or "Can I get new sneakers?" or "How many dimes make a dollar?" Not infrequently, bedtime comes on the heels of an epic sibling throwdown, a Chernobyl-esque emotional meltdown, or just garden-variety bad behavior ("I'm *not* tired!"). On those occasions, I ad-lib. "And, God, please help Charley to remember that biting his sister is wrong," or "Dear Lord, help Vale not to sass, to be gentle and kind with her words." It's prayer, with an agenda. It reminds me of the story Jesus told about how the Pharisees pray.

"Two men went to the Temple to pray. One was a Pharisee, and the other was a despised tax collector. The Pharisee stood by himself and prayed this prayer: 'I thank you, God, that I am not like other people—cheaters, sinners, adulterers. I'm certainly not like that tax collector! I fast twice a week, and I give you a tenth of my income.'"

Luke 18:10–12 NLT

Gotta love this guy! *Thank you, Lord, that I'm not like all those much more wretched people!* We could have a good, hearty laugh at those silly Pharisees if we weren't so often exactly like them. When we are struggling with someone, when we are in conflict or feel hurt or anger toward those closest to us, our prayers can take on that tenor. "Please, God, help Joe come to see why he is wrong"; "I pray, Lord, you would help Maggie with her tendencies toward self-centeredness and victimhood"; or "May you grant Aunt Bev a new perspective and supernatural wisdom [. . . so she can start agreeing with me]." Major Pharisee vibes.

If the subjects of our prayers were acquaintances or casual work colleagues, it wouldn't be an issue. Because we probably wouldn't be praying at all. But we often turn to prayer in desperation, when we find ourselves in conflict with the people we most care about, our hearts and souls plagued by the struggle. These are the hard cases, the most fraught situations, the ones that gnaw at us the most. In other words: family (usually). Husbands, wives, mothers, fathers, sisters, brothers, aunts, uncles, cousins, in-laws—pick your poison. The long history, the shared traumas, the depth of connection, and the gravity of the emotional stakes—that's what makes these pains so persistent and so impossible to ignore. It's at these times we need prayer the most. And often when we find it hardest to do.

My sister is by far the most wise, intelligent, thoughtful, creative, generous, and profoundly original person I know. She is my forever partner in life. We know each other's thoughts and ways. We know each other's sadnesses and weaknesses. We know each other's tickle spots and pain points. Vastly different on the surface but fundamentally alike—both manifesting the childhood we share in our own individual ways.

In her memoir, writer and Bible teacher Beth Moore said she and her siblings had "different slices of the same secrets . . . on our plates."[1] Annie and I have different slices of the same heartbreaks on ours.

Sometimes the way we have found each other in the hard times is God, the sixth member of our family, as my sister so memorably put it. I know when she is praying for me, and I believe she knows when I am praying for her too. The result is some holy alchemy, God bringing us together, not always by the immediate resolution of our conflict, but by stitching us back together in the most eternal way. God sends us to our spiritual room together, and we find each other in the dark. When we pray for each another, we know and believe deeply that our intentions toward each another are good, our foundation is love, we have integrity in our struggles, we are willing to look at our own wrongs, and we are committed to our relationship for the long term. For eternity.

Author Shauna Niequist wrote about conflict and prayer in her book *I Guess I Haven't Learned That Yet.*[2] Shauna and I attend the same church in New York City, and I once heard her give a sermon on the subject. She said something that changed how I think about prayer: When you don't have words, use what you do have. Pray with your imagination.

Sometimes when my feelings betray me, when I feel distant or angry or afraid to be vulnerable, when words are beyond me, I pray with my imagination. I imagine my children at peace and content. Secure. Not fighting! I imagine my husband fulfilled and at peace. I picture his face and set him in a tranquil surrounding. Or I picture my beautiful sister—serene, smiling, laughing. I picture her surrounded by nature, where I know she feels most at home and

In those hard
moments, God
can be the way we
find our path back
to each other.

centered. Or climbing a mountain, standing at the top, marveling at the beauty, some poem at its moment of conception in her gorgeous mind.

There is no agenda to these prayers other than the joy I feel conjuring my loved ones' joy, summoning their sweet presence in my mind. I don't know if they can feel it, and I don't know if it changes anything for them, but it changes me. Shauna said it's like yoga when you breathe into a stretch and find you can go further than you thought you could go.[3]

Love washes over me, my heart softens, my fears dissipate. The atmosphere is changed. Words cannot express it. It is, in every respect, divine.

PSALM 23

When I was about ten or so, I went to stay at my cousins' house for a week. They lived in another land— Phoenix!—about a two-hour drive north from my hometown of Tucson, Arizona. My first cousin Teri Stauffer is my father's niece, but we are about twenty years apart, so she was always more like an aunt to me. Her three kids, Paige, Charley, and Holly, are my second cousins, much closer to my age. They are like a set of extra siblings to me. We all grew up together, our families trading weekends at each other's houses, spending long days in the pool, playing dress-up, making up plays, or darting around the desert, our little knees scratched and bleeding from frequent close encounters with cacti and our noses pink from the scorching sun.

About once a year, in the summertime, Cousin Teri orchestrated a "kidnapping" of my sister and me. It went down like this: The cousins would visit for a few days at our house in Tucson, and then, on the morning they were to leave, Teri would wake us up early, shushing us in the predawn darkness as we made our escape. We would all pile into her rickety station wagon and head north, the sky streaking with bright oranges and pinks as the sun rose over the colorless desert landscape. Somewhere between Phoenix and Tucson, Teri would make a pit stop and let Annie and me call home at a pay phone. "Mom! Cousin Teri kidnapped us to take us to her house!" My mother would feign shock, protest how terribly she would miss us, then assure us she'd drive up to retrieve us in a few days.

Our two families were close in every sense: in geography, in relationship, and in faith—the tie that bound us most deeply of all. We had sort of spiritual parallel lives: churchgoers, choir members, Sunday school volunteers, Bible study teachers. (At one point, the whole Stauffer family moved to Brazil to plant a church and became full-time missionaries. Another story for another time.)

Teri's three kids, my cousins, were a few years younger than my sister and me, and on those "kidnapping" adventures she could sometimes default into assuming Annie and I were more mature and grown up than we really were. One time, I burst into tears at the breakfast table after Teri, cutting her kids' food, bypassed our plates. "Why are you crying?" she asked, startled.

"My mommy cuts *my* pancakes at home!" I said.

She smiled and squeezed me. "I'm so sorry! Sometimes I forget that you're still little too!"

I was about five years old then. But as the years went on and the treasured summer tradition continued, I came to love feeling a bit more grown up, being independent of my parents; it was part of the magic of being away. I have memories of quietly observing as Teri busily completed her morning tasks. One of her beloved rituals was her coffee break with the neighbor across the street. Sometimes she let me tag along. I can still see us sitting around Najwa's kitchen table, sipping "coffee" (mostly warm milk in a mug for me), the adults conversing. Their conversation was beyond me, but I loved hanging with the ladies.

It was on one of those mornings that Teri introduced me to Psalm 23—a passage that I will carry with me for the rest of my life. She handed me her Bible and told me to look it up and memorize it. I was intrigued and a tiny bit proud. To me, it was her way of saying, "I think you're old enough to handle this"—a vote of confidence in my mind and my heart.

To this day, I don't know why she chose that particular passage. Psalm 23 is famous, I later learned, but it isn't easy. It is intimidatingly long for a kid's "memory verse," and to top it off, the version she gave me came from the old King James Bible, with its ancient and alienating *thys* and *thees*, its *maketh*s and *runneth*s and *anointeth*s.

The LORD is my shepherd; I shall not want.
He maketh me to lie down in green pastures: he
leadeth me beside the still waters.
He restoreth my soul: he leadeth me in the paths of
righteousness for his name's sake.
Yea, though I walk through the valley of the shadow
of death, I will fear no evil: for thou art with
me; thy rod and thy staff they comfort me.
Thou preparest a table before me in the presence
of mine enemies: thou anointest my head with
oil; my cup runneth over.
Surely goodness and mercy shall follow me all the
days of my life: and I will dwell in the house of
the LORD forever.

Psalm 23 KJV

The meaning of this long passage was oblique and mostly impenetrable to me. "I shall not want"—huh? "Thou anointest my head with oil" . . . sounded unpleasant. Yet I accepted the challenge. I memorized the words I could barely comprehend. And, inexplicably, they stuck with me.

Psalm 23 is my psalm. It is my friend and my helper: a gift that God gave me as a child and has let me rediscover, year after year, always finding something new beneath the surface. It is like a gem that unexpectedly catches the light, revealing brilliant new facets and colors.

And Psalm 23 is our secret code, God and me. Sometimes, in moments of need, it appears out of nowhere—a little Post-it Note from above. The first time my pastor asked me to speak at our church, a sermon of sorts, I was terrified and intimidated, the ultimate impostor. Lo and behold, the hymn chosen by the music leader that morning? A musical adaptation of Psalm 23. I smiled to myself. Message received, in a way only God and I would understand. *I am here. I am with you.*

It is like a gem that unexpectedly catches the light, revealing brilliant new facets and colors.

But really, Psalm 23 is everybody's psalm. It is famous for a reason, holding interest and relevance across time and generations, capable of interpretation and reinterpretation. It is the Bible's *Mona Lisa*; walk a few steps to the side of it and you may see it in an entirely different light. Whole books have been dedicated to its captivating passages.

The Lord is my shepherd; I shall not want.

Every need we have is met—by God himself.

He makes me lie down in green pastures; he leads me beside quiet waters.

Our physical need—for food, water, sustenance—is met.

He refreshes my soul; he guides me along the right paths for his name's sake.

Our spiritual need—for meaning and purpose—is met.

Even though I walk through the darkest valley, I will fear no evil, for you are with me; your rod and staff, they comfort me.

Our need for safety is met.

You prepare a table before me in the presence of my enemies.

Our need for identity is met—the chosen of God!

My cup overflows.

Our need for perspective is met.

Surely your goodness and love will follow me all the days of my life.

Our need for hope is met.

And I will dwell in the house of the Lord forever.

Our need for eternity is met.

At its essence, Psalm 23 is a passage of rest. I find reciting the Shepherd's Psalm on a sleepless night to be far superior to counting sheep. In those long, dark hours of tossing and turning, the dread of the approaching alarm growing heavier with every glance at the clock, I summon my psalm in desperation. I recite it to myself, retracing its long, meandering byways in my mind. It may take a few cycles as my thoughts inevitably wander into concerns and distractions. But gently, I nudge myself back to the words, like a shepherd coaxing a lost sheep home again. And inevitably, sleep comes.

Other times, wide awake and beset by anxiety, I turn to it for meditation, a way to train my focus on something other than my worries and fears. Have you ever noticed how mundane concerns can take on outsized proportion when we lie in our beds, at our most vulnerable? Ordinary things—like whether to make cupcakes homemade or just do store-bought for my kid's birthday party—can take on agonizing importance in the dark of night. In the morning, I wake up and wonder, *What the heck was that all about?* (And: store-bought, obviously!)

On nights like those, sometimes I close my eyes and draw out each line of my psalm, diverting my anxious thoughts by visualizing each scene: the grassy field, the trickling stream. I conjure in my mind a bright blue sky, the feel of solid earth under me, a gentle breeze and the warmth of the sun upon my face. The tranquil opening scenes of Psalm 23 are a lovely space to invite an uneasy mind to sit for a spell.

———

These images are deeply part of me now; they have come to represent the very presence of God, what it must look like and feel like. This serene and quiet place is my spiritual home base. And I have come to see that the psalm offers a rest deeper than the physical, far more than a momentary reprieve from exhaustion. It speaks to a respite from the human condition itself.

True, spiritual rest comes when we do not feel frantic and desperate to care for ourselves, grasping and hoarding out of a sense of scarcity and fear. True rest comes when we know who we are: the beloved and cared-for of God himself. Put another way, this psalm is saying: *You can relax now. Lay down your labors and exertions; for God is here, present and providing.*

My daughter was born in 2014, and we decided not to find out the baby's gender. For some reason, however, we just assumed it was a boy and never really considered girls' names. Imagine our surprise when out she came and the doctor declared, "It's a girl!" Delighted, overjoyed, and me a little foggy from the painkillers, we had to come up with a girl's name—quickly. A long time ago, I had heard the name Vale in passing and always loved it. Miraculously, Mike liked it too. Unusual but dignified, not too trendy or distracting—she could be a poet or a secretary of state with such a name. Vale it was.

> True rest comes when we know who we are: the beloved and cared-for of God himself.

I didn't know much about the word's origin, other than it was an old, no-longer-much-used English word that meant, in essence, "peaceful valley." I later saw it turn up in old hymns at church ("field and forest, vale and mountain . . . praising you eternally!")[1] and was delighted. But only recently—years after her birth!—did it dawn on me that her name evoked the very images of Psalm 23 I have always treasured. What is the peaceful, grassy field alongside still waters if not a vale?

Isn't God interesting?

———

I ran across a gem tucked in the pages of an old journal, scrawled messily on loose-leaf notepad paper (emblazoned with my law firm's logo, of all things, identifying it as likely written circa 2003).

Psalm 23 in my own words:

God himself is taking care of me; my every need is met. He causes me to relax, rest, give up control, and feel his comfort, like cool grass, envelop me. Where he takes me, peace can be found; he shows me tranquility and calm. He gives back to me all that the world has taken; he lovingly patches the pieces of my heart. He goes ahead of me, carving a path of goodness and rightness, worn by his own footsteps and tested with his very presence. He sets out a path that will give my life meaning, by letting me be a credit to his name. Even when I look at death itself, or face a life of darkness and despair, doubt and fear, I will be miraculously delivered: confident in spite of circumstances, triumphant even when things crumble around me. I think of God's vast power, his life-giving, earth-creating, universe-holding power, and I am comforted that he who holds the world also holds me. God has showered his favor on me, blessed me lavishly, embarrassed me with riches of every kind. He has selected me, chosen me out of the crowd, and loved me extravagantly—out in front for all the world to see. I have too many blessings to count and am filled with love for the one who has blessed me. Because of this, because God has shown his love and devotion to me, because he has saved me for no other reason than that he can, and because he saves me daily and carries me through this life, I am confident that he will not abandon me and that his goodness, kindness, grace, and compassion also will be with me all of my days. And I know he will welcome me home, daughter returning to Father, to find he has saved a space for me and invited me to stay forever.

God's words are meant for this: to be tasted, lingered over, and savored. His words are meant to be ingested and absorbed into our bloodstream. They're meant to become part of us. Whatever your "Psalm 23" is—a scripture, a quote, a song—if it speaks to your soul, God is likely speaking to you.

> God's word is not a reference book in a library that we pull off the shelf when we want information. There is nothing inert or bookish in these words. God's words . . . hit us where we live. The moment we know this, that God speaks to us, delight is spontaneous.[2]
> **Eugene Peterson,** *Living the Message*

True, spiritual rest comes
when we do not feel frantic and
desperate to care for ourselves,
grasping and hoarding out of a
sense of scarcity and fear.

CHAPTER 12

A BEAUTIFUL DAY IN THE NEIGHBORHOOD

A movie about Mister Rogers came out a few years back. Tom Hanks portrayed the cardigan-clad maestro of nice. (Perfect casting if there ever was.) It was mostly the tale of how the mild-mannered pastor from Pittsburgh became the public television juggernaut and American icon.

I remember watching Mister Rogers when I was little. I liked how he tossed his sneakers in the air as he changed his shoes and how his cardigans were all lined up neatly in the hall closet. I enjoyed the land of make-believe and that postman who was always stopping by.

Ironically, one of my earliest (and somewhat painful) memories involves Mister Rogers. I was in half-day kindergarten, my siblings still at school, when one afternoon, my mom, trying to assuage my boredom, offered to turn on *Mister Rogers' Neighborhood* on the living room TV. I can still see that old, clunky TV, its two spiky antennae pointed wonkily left and right, one knob for volume, one to turn the channel. Ah, the good old days when you had to literally walk across the room to change the channel, which is probably why my sister and I often sprawled out on the rug about three inches in front of the set. "Girls!" my mother would shriek. "Move back! You're going to ruin your eyes!" But I digress.

Little did my mother know that her kind offer produced a deep, overwhelming feeling of sadness and grief in me. *I'm too old for Mister Rogers*, I thought. *But Mommy doesn't know that. She still thinks I'm a baby.* I felt sad and sorry for her and guilty that she didn't realize I was growing up. So I went along and told her I really, really wanted to watch it. (Therapists, rev your engines.) Isn't it funny the moments we remember from childhood?

Anyway.

Everyone knows Mister Rogers as a gentle presence and thoughtful educator, but he was also a man of devout faith—a Presbyterian minister by training. A creature of fastidious habits and practices, Mister Rogers had a regular prayer routine. He prayed for the people he knew, every day, by name.

Right about now you're thinking, *Great, thanks. Reason number*

Praying their names feels
like an act of love, an act of
meaning, and an act of hope.
Lifting up the people I love
before the God I trust draws
me closer to him and to them.

ten billion why I will never be as saintly as Mister Rogers. I yell at my children and definitely don't pray daily for every person in my life.

That's what I would think if I hadn't seen a remarkable scene in the movie *A Beautiful Day in the Neighborhood* of Mister Rogers, kneeling by his bed, hands folded, head bowed, reciting names.[1]

Cecilia Sherman.

Colby Dickerson.

And on it would go. You get the picture.

That's all. No narrative. No backstory. No requests. No explanations. Just . . . names. One after the other.

The idea is moving and powerful. And instructive. We may genuinely want to pray for others—our friends, families, coworkers, leaders. But the sheer volume is overwhelming, let alone any attempt to capture every need. And sometimes, prayers for others can become freighted with emotion. Mixed motives. Prescriptions. Judgments. Even when our intentions start off in a good place, it is easy to veer off course.

WWMRD? What would Mister Rogers do?

Some mornings, I pray names, just names, just like he did. I whisper my husband's name to God and picture his image. Mike. Then my kids. Vale. Charley. I imagine them one by one, summoning their sweet faces. Mom, Annie, Cam. I see them in my mind. This prayer experience is surprisingly powerful; it bonds us deeply to the ones whose names we utter, softening any edges. Praying their names feels like an act of love, an act of meaning, and an act of hope. Lifting up the people I love before the God I trust draws me closer to him and to them.

When time is short, lives are harried, minds are distracted, and our internal dialogues are burdened, we can say their names, trusting that God will take it from there.

PART 3

PRAISE

CHAPTER 13

GARMENT OF PRAISE

W ho are you wearing?"

I've covered a few red carpets in my day. It's wild. You stand, squeezed tight into a packed scrum of other reporters (and usually squeezed tight into your dress), and wait/hope for celebrity A-listers to grace you with their absurdly attractive presence for a hot second. The pre-event scene at the big awards shows like the Emmys or Golden Globes is especially chaotic. Publicists squire impossibly thin and luminous clients down a gauntlet of live cameras, as ravenous network producers flag them over—hands outstretched grade-school style ("Over here, over here, over here!")—hoping one of the uber-fabulous will deign to stop. These sought-after "interviews" last anywhere from thirty to ninety seconds. It is like speed dating, with even less chance of a genuine interaction.

The single question, ringing out again and again, as ubiquitous on red carpets as Botox and hunger pangs: "Who are you wearing?" It's all part of the celebrity economy, of course. The stars get to borrow gorgeous clothes with the understanding that they will mention the designer at every available opportunity. Win-win!

> "Who are you wearing?" A shallow, vapid question. But what if it is a penetrating spiritual question?

Personally, I've never loved the question (and yes, I've asked it plenty). Aside from the crime against grammar, who really cares if the dress is Prada or PUCCI or Proenza? I like pretty things as much as anyone (and the outfits are the only reason to watch these red-carpet specials), but wouldn't you rather know why they chose that particular gown? How many they tried on? If they're wearing SPANX, and if so, how many pairs? Something—anything—more interesting than name-dropping a designer brand we can't pronounce.

"Who are you wearing?" A shallow, vapid question. But what if it is a penetrating spiritual question?

> The Spirit of the Sovereign LORD . . . has sent
> me . . . to comfort all who mourn . . .
> to bestow on them a crown of beauty
> instead of ashes . . . a garment of praise
> instead of a spirit of despair.
>
> Isaiah 61:1–3

A garment of praise. What a treasure buried in a long, famous passage from Isaiah.

But let me back up a bit.

> Give praise to the LORD, proclaim his name.
>
> Isaiah 12:4

"Praise the Lord." This exhortation is shot throughout the Scriptures. Old Testament and New, whatever translation you favor, you will see it time and again.

> For great is the LORD and most worthy of praise!
>
> 1 Chronicles 16:25

> Let us continually offer to God a sacrifice of praise.
>
> Hebrews 13:15

Praise be to the God and Father of our Lord Jesus Christ, who has blessed us in the heavenly realms with every spiritual blessing in Christ.

Ephesians 1:3

And we haven't even gotten to the Psalms!

Exalt the LORD our God and worship at his footstool.

Psalm 99:5

Let everything that has breath praise the LORD.

Psalm 150:6

I will extol the LORD at all times; his praise will always be on my lips.

Psalm 34:1

Praise the LORD, my soul; all my inmost being, praise his holy name.

Psalm 103:1

Give praise to the LORD, proclaim his name; make known among the nations what he has done.

Psalm 105:1

> Praise the LORD, you his angels, you mighty
> ones who do his bidding, who obey his
> word. Praise the LORD, all his heavenly
> hosts, you his servants who do his will.
> Praise the LORD, all his works everywhere
> in his dominion. Praise the LORD, my soul.
>
> Psalm 103:20–22

Okay! Message received.

I probably shouldn't admit this, especially in a book about faith, but at times I have wondered to myself—secretly—*Uhhhh, what's with all the requests for praise? Why is God always asking for compliments? Is he angling for credit? Is our God cosmically and eternally needy?*

This irreverent thought jiggled around in the back of my mind for a long time, though I was too ashamed to really confront it. But of course, God knows the content of our hearts. So when I came across that phrase from Isaiah—"garment of praise"—it leaped off the page.

Garment.

Suddenly, I got it. If praise is a garment, who is wearing it? We are. We are ones who are adorned. God tells us to praise him not for what it does for him but for what it does for us.

Lightning bolt.

When we count our blessings and remember what we are thankful for and what is good in our lives, we are the beneficiaries. It lifts our spirits and fills us with joy.

It's yet another example of "mostly what God does is love us," this call to praise. Because God knows that when we can bring ourselves

If praise is a garment, who is wearing it? We are. We are the ones who are adorned. God tells us to praise him not for what it does for him but for what it does for us.

---

to a place of gratitude, to look beyond ourselves and to him, it is a profound benefit to our hearts, our souls, and our persons. Sure, God, as the object of our affection, is praised as well, but we are the ones who are enhanced, heartened, and changed by the act.

> How good it is to sing praises to our God, how
> pleasant and fitting to praise him!
>
> Psalm 147:1

He calls for praise—not to fill his deep need but to fill ours. It is we who are dressed in that beautiful garment of praise.

So . . . who are you wearing?

———

I once heard gratitude referred to as the "low-hanging fruit" of well-being. Interesting. But that suggests finding gratitude is easy, and sometimes, it's not. Sometimes finding gratitude feels like you're scaling Half Dome in Yosemite, not picking up a peach that just fell fortuitously to the ground. It feels like it takes supreme effort from within.

If you're of a certain era and religious upbringing, perhaps you've heard of a woman named Joni Eareckson Tada. My mother admired her and read her books in the 1980s. I distinctly remember my mom telling the young teenage me about Joni—probably as both a spiritual inspiration and a cautionary tale. Joni was just seventeen years old, an athletic young girl from Maryland, when she dove into shallow water and broke her neck. She was immediately paralyzed from the neck down—quadriplegic. Joni has since lived a beautiful, honest life of faith and service. (And creativity! She paints beautiful canvases using a paintbrush nestled between her teeth. Extraordinary.)

Years later, well into my adulthood, I came across an interview with her on *Larry King Live*.[1] Remembering her from my youth, I stopped and watched. She told the story of how she came to faith. She said she had not been a particularly devout person before her accident, and in the excruciating weeks and months after, lying prostrate in her hospital bed, the buoyant life she imagined cruelly snatched away, her despair grew so unbearable she wished for death. She even tried to accomplish it—to break her neck again, right there in her hospital bed. Her paralysis left her unable to complete the task.

Joni told a story about the moment everything changed for her. Some family friends had come to her hospital room to cheer her up. They supplied pizza and watched NCAA football and, as she says, "treated me as a human being,"[2] not an invalid. They also brought their Bibles. Though she wasn't very religious, Joni said their kindness earned them the right to open them. The verse that changed her life was this one:

> Give thanks in all circumstances; for this is God's will for you in Christ Jesus.
>
> 1 Thessalonians 5:18

I sat watching, astonished. I couldn't believe this was the verse that had so deeply affected her. It wasn't a verse of encouragement. It wasn't even a verse promising a better life in eternity. It gave nothing to her; on the contrary, it asked something. It was calling Joni to gratitude, someone from whom so much had been taken. Give thanks? Seriously?

And yet that is exactly what turned her life around. Joni herself said she didn't understand it right away. She didn't spend every waking moment from that day forward in a state of radiant rapture. Life was hard. Someone still had to lift her out of bed, bathe her, feed her. Some days it took all she had to go on. But somehow, praise and gratitude were her most potent healer. And she said that the weaker she felt, the more unable to do it, the stronger God became.

Wherever you are in this moment and however you feel, if you want to immediately alter the atmosphere, if you want to instantly change the air, praise him.

———

Praise. Gratitude. Thanksgiving.

Wherever you are in this moment and however you feel, if you want to immediately alter the atmosphere, if you want to instantly change the air, praise him.

I like the old King James translation of Psalm 22:3: "O thou that inhabitest the praises of Israel." He inhabits the praises of his people.

If you're wondering where God is, praise him. Suddenly, you will be in his presence. We've already learned his phone number. If you're looking for his address, this is where he lives.

CHAPTER 14

TURN YOUR
EYES

I was sitting in my cozy chair, before dawn, enveloped in my blanket, reading the day's briefing material for work, when I heard the pitter-patter of little footsteps on the stairs. Just kidding. What I actually heard were the thunderous thuds of a boxing heavyweight lumbering down the steps as though hoisting a grand piano. In other words, the footsteps of an eight-year-old. Sure enough, it was Vale, up early, looking for me. I was already running late for work, but I couldn't resist gathering her into my arms for a quiet moment before the bustle of the day began. I nestled her into my lap, pulling her curly head to my chest as we said a prayer for the day to come. Quiet. Still. All alone—just us. How I hold these moments in my heart; soon my grade-school angel will be a teenager, maybe a snarly one, not so willing to be cradled by her mommy.

"Mom," she said, looking up at me as our prayer ended. "Sometimes I can feel the earth move." I paused, waiting for more. She went on. "You know how the earth moves around the sun? Sometimes I can feel it moving. I can see the clouds going across the sky."

I smiled. I told her it was pretty cool that she could do that. She scampered off.

Heavenly perspective. It is as rare and precious as stolen moments with our children in the dark before dawn.

We can't really feel the turn of the earth, of course. There are probably many good scientific reasons for that (I assume?). But there is also a spiritual reason we so rarely perceive the cosmic, divine movement around us. We are not quiet, we are not still, we are not alone—just us—with God. And we are not looking in the right place. On most days we are looking inward, outward, or a combination of both. Horizontal, not vertical. We are not looking toward the heavens.

We are only human, after all. Our default gaze is earthward. Our default focus is inward: our needs, our wants, our families, our comings and goings. Our jobs, our health, our dreams, our pleasures. It is all about us. Perspective does not come naturally. Like children, to whom "please," "excuse me," and "thank you" must be taught, we, too, have to learn. We, too, have to practice.

Like so many people, I struggle with dark and foreboding thoughts. I don't know if mine has a clinical name—anxiety, perhaps? No matter—I don't need to name it; I know it by heart. I would know it anywhere. That heavy feeling of dread, worry, and guilt gripping my heart like a vise. The tightening, gnawing feeling of discomfort, unease. It is dis-ease, if not an actual disease. A persistent, occasionally relentless sense of impending doom.

Its defining feature is its mystery—why do I feel this way? Often, I can't even put my finger on it. I rack my brain for the source, scanning my memory, movements, and interactions—looking for the real reason I might feel so unsettled. Did I do something wrong? Have I hurt someone inadvertently? Am I acting in a way that invites terrible consequences? Am I out on a dangerous limb in any way that God doesn't approve of? Why do I feel I am in trouble? That some cosmic condemnation is about to come down on me, that calamity is always around the corner?

These feelings are a mountain to overcome—sometimes, a daily climb. I try to smile my way past them at work and at home. I keep going; I keep my worry to myself. But inside, these feelings are a festering rot—a killer of joy and robber of peace. I'm sure there are answers in my brain chemistry and my childhood for these feelings—fertile ground for a mental health professional. And yes, I have and will continue to explore those worthy avenues.

> Our default gaze is earthward. Our default focus is inward: our needs, our wants, our families, our comings and goings.

But what I also know, deeply, is that I need perspective. Not just "This too shall pass," "Count your blessings," or "Focus on the positive." I need to place myself and my worries in a larger context. Specifically, a divine one. Only in the context of God can I have any real perspective at all.

Rick Warren, author of *The Purpose Driven Life*, said, "Worry is the warning light that God has been shoved to the sideline."[1] It surely is. Usually, what displaces God is the world, everything down here. All the distractions, all the concerns. This observation is not meant to pile on the guilt, more fodder for a further beatdown. God made us. He knows we are human. "He remembers that we are dust," as the scripture says (Psalm 103:14). Yet things are better when our gazes are thrust beyond ourselves, higher, fixed upon the eternal. We cannot possess that perspective all the time. But when we do, it is an extraordinary gift.

> Things are better when our gazes are thrust beyond ourselves, higher, fixed upon the eternal.

I lift up my eyes to the mountains—
where does my help come from? My help
comes from the LORD,
the Maker of heaven and earth.

Psalm 121:1–2

I prayed this psalm on the first day I ever hosted the *TODAY Show*. It was a Monday morning in mid-July 2012. I was a bit nervous, by which I mean utterly terrified. I had started my new job during a time of great difficulty for the show. I was given the position hurriedly and unexpectedly, amid controversy; I was certain I would not last long before the bosses realized they had chosen wrong or the audience rejected me. I felt the scrutinizing eyes of the world upon me. I think I barely ate for a week before that first show. Proving that stress will manifest in the body, I even came down with a blinding migraine that first morning. It was so bad I had to lie down on my office floor with the lights out twenty minutes before air. The producers and other anchors gently knocked on the door to see if I was going to make it.

I prayed, of course. And at some point, God gave me that scripture. I had memorized it years prior (during one of those seasons of devout Bible study I told you about!). Suddenly, the words popped into my memory—just in the nick of time, just when I needed it. *I lift up my eyes to the mountains.* I felt a flush of safety, of confidence—not in myself but in him. *Where does my help come from? My help comes from the Lord, the Maker of heaven and earth.* Relief. God is with me. He's got me. I am not alone. Whatever happens, I will never be alone. He has brought me to this moment, and he is not about to abandon me now.

Great wisdom and great comfort come from doing what the psalmist suggested: look up, look out, look to the beyond. And what do we see? Help on the way—coming from the hills and high places. Rescue. Hosanna in the highest. We see God—who he is, his essence, his character, his methods. We see him in charge and in control. We see him focused and paying attention. We see him:

God is with me. He's got me. I am not alone. Whatever happens, I will never be alone. He has brought me to this moment, and he is not about to abandon me now.

Maker, Creator, Author, Provider—on earth as it is in heaven. God is there and he is good. Perspective. The heavenly kind.

When anxious thoughts overwhelm me, when negativity harasses me, it is a sure sign I have forgotten all of that. I have forgotten who God is and what he promises. I must look up. I must look for him. When my spirit fails, I must look to the heavens for these truths.

God is the judge of my flaws, and he promises mercy.

God is in charge of my safety and protection, and he promises eternal life.

God is the guardian of my heart and well-being, and he shows tenderness and loving-kindness to all he has made—including me.

When my son, Charley, was two years old, he threw a toy train at me. It wasn't intentional. It was a classic toddler science experiment: What happens if I hurl this sharp object toward my mother's face? Answer: it will hurt. This was an absurdly heavy toy with an absurdly pointy, old-fashioned cowcatcher at the front. Fun for toddlers and perfect for eye gouging, which it did. (Tangent: we actually kept the train for years afterward, and the kids referred to it as The Weapon.)

Long story short, the locomotive projectile caused a massive tear in my retina, and I briefly lost vision in one eye. I had multiple surgeries, including one in which I had to spend an entire week face down for hours upon hours in the day (and night). I rented one of those massage chairs you see at the nail salon and buried my head downward. I read books and listened to podcasts. I bought a little hand mirror that I tilted up so I could see my children's faces. I spent long hours face down in that chair. It was boring. It was lonely. It was painful (when you're constantly looking down, your neck hurts). You miss eye contact. You miss smiles. You miss connection.

Metaphor alert. When we are looking down, looking inward too much, we miss so much. A friend's father-in-law has the same birthday wish every year. When he blows out the candles and the grandkids ask, "What did you ask for?" his answer is always the same: "I asked for perspective." What a wise birthday wish (I'm stealing it).

> When we are looking down, looking inward too much, we miss so much.

Look, I live in the real world too. We can't walk around in a state of beatific rhapsody at all times. (I would literally run into things—especially with that bad eye.) But fixing our gazes heavenward, lifting up our eyes, is sensible and practical. Our spirits have peripheral vision just as our eyes do. We know what transpires around us and how to navigate. But with a heavenly perspective, we will not be consumed. We will not be overwhelmed. For when we look to the heavens, we see God—looking right back at us.

I love this old hymn from my childhood:

> *Turn your eyes upon Jesus,*
> *Look full on his wonderful face.*
> *And the things of earth will grow strangely dim,*
> *In the light of his glory and grace.*[2]

When our hearts are troubled, may we pray to be able to look up and outward. May we pray for a vantage point that spans time and space, that processes the meaning of things not across moments but across millennia. A God's-eye view.

[Jesus] looked toward heaven and prayed.

John 17:1

CHAPTER 15

UNSUBSCRIBING FROM MYSELF

E very year, starting in my late twenties and continuing for the better part of a decade, my mom bought me the same Christmas gift. She dutifully wrapped it up, but it was easy to identify under the tree by its consistent size, shape, and weight: a fresh, shiny, plastic-wrapped journal called *Journeying Through the Days*. It wasn't her only Christmas gift, mind you—she also would've gotten me the boots or designer jeans I asked for or the acoustic guitar I didn't know I wanted (my mom is an amazingly intuitive gift giver!). But this was our tradition, our special thing, our bond. It was how she encouraged/reminded/prodded me to walk with God as I walked into adulthood.

My mom had been writing in these very same journals for years, chronicling her hopes and revelations, disappointments and worries. I can still see her messy cursive filling up every corner of the page. She wrote faithfully every day. Sometimes I was tempted to sneak a peek, to get some insight into the deepest part of her, but I never did. Snooping into this sacred, private space would have been a violation. That, and I was a little afraid of what I might discover there.

These were Christian journals. Each day of the week had a chosen scripture as a prompt and a blank section for reflection. The other pages were filled out with serene nature photographs and inspirational quotes. That's the reason, I suppose, that the journals became a spiritual diary for me. There are no logs of the day's comings and goings or recounting of personal happenings at work or school or dating (thankfully!). They are an extended, raw, honest, and often wrenching conversation with God. I guess you could call them prayers.

God tells us to "pour out [our] hearts to him" (Psalm 62:8). I definitely took him up on it.

Free me from my despair that I have messed up my life beyond repair. Help me, save me. That's all I ask, and it is everything. Free me. Save me. Lead me. Show me. I am incapable of clarity.

I cringe to reread my words now. My self-centeredness and lack of perspective is a *wow* (and not in a good way). But God isn't looking for perfect words or pious exaltations. He isn't looking for posturing or pretense. He is looking for the mess. In other words, he is looking for us.

He isn't looking for posturing or pretense. He is looking for the mess. In other words, he is looking for us.

Journals are a place to let it all hang out: the good, the bad, the ugly, and the even uglier. God invites us not to deny or ignore our feelings but to process them in his presence.

I believe there is nothing we can't say to God. In fact, I am sure of it because I've read the Psalms, a tour de force of despondency, fear, frustration, anxiety, panic, anger, and wrath. In a way, they were a "journal" of sorts.

> I am overwhelmed with troubles
>> and my life draws near to death.
> I am counted among those who go down to the pit;
>> I am like one without strength.
> I am set apart with the dead,
>> like the slain who lie in the grave,
> whom you remember no more,
>> who are cut off from your care.
> You have put me in the lowest pit,
>> in the darkest depths.
> Your wrath lies heavily on me;
>> you have overwhelmed me with all your
>>> waves.

You have taken from me my closest friends
and have made me repulsive to them.
I am confined and cannot escape;
my eyes are dim with grief. . . .
Why, LORD, do you reject me
and hide your face from me?
From my youth I have suffered and been close
to death;
I have borne your terrors and am in despair.
Your wrath has swept over me;
your terrors have destroyed me.
All day long they surround me like a flood;
they have completely engulfed me.
You have taken from me friend and neighbor—
darkness is my closest friend.

Psalm 88:3–9, 14–18

Sometimes it's good to read the Psalms just to feel better about our own level of drama and navel-gazing.

I kept my journals going for a decade or longer. But at some point, *Journeying Through the Days* stopped being published, and my mom's little Christmas tradition died. For a while, I kept it up here and there, scribbling in notebooks, but then I stopped writing pretty much altogether.

It wasn't a coincidence. I was busy, trying to make my way at my new job at NBC. And my personal life was falling apart disastrously. I was barely holding on. No time to probe the depths of my soul, and nothing good to find there, anyway. I signed off from myself. *Unsubscribe.* I packed the journals away in a box, put them in an attic (another metaphor alert!), and did not look at or think of them for years. Not forgotten, but I was on the move.

Life went on. Years went by. I moved to New York City, started a new job at *TODAY*, got married, had two kids. Who has time to sit around harvesting old journals for self-discovery? And even if I found the time—not unlike how I felt about my mom's journals—I was a little afraid of what I might discover there.

But recently, I decided to trudge up the stairs and blow the dust off the plastic bin. I began to read.

It was . . . a lot. The Ghost of Savannah Past, a multivolume series of angst and torment, a guided tour through inadequacy, loneliness, fear, and confession. And, above all, guilt. So. Much. Guilt. Guilt for being distracted, for being shallow, for being ambitious. Guilt for blending in with the crowd, for not being more forward in my faith. Guilt for not writing in my journal. Guilt for not saying my prayers or doing my Bible study. Guilt for ignoring God when times were good, then crawling back when heartbreak inevitably called. Guilt for not keeping his commands. Guilt for not *wanting* to keep his commands.

A lifetime ago. I had forgotten so much. I forgot how I used to feel, how much I used to be afraid of God. I wanted to please him and follow his path, but I deeply suspected that his master plan for me would lead to "humiliation and painful lessons" (actual journal quote). Motivated by that fear, I strived to be a good girl and stay on the straight and narrow.

Of course, piety or perfection were far too difficult for me. I hoped to be just passable enough that God's discipline would pass over me, that he would have worse cases to deal with. As long as I stayed just this side of "not great but not that bad," he would not chasten me or take away some comfort I enjoyed or success I craved. I was trying to control God, this powerful and terrifying force. I might pay lip service to his goodness and mercy, and many mornings I would genuinely and joyfully sing his praises, but in actuality, day after day, my writing belied my true feelings: a sneaking suspicion that whatever God wanted or planned for me, it would be painful or sacrificial or unpleasant. It is uniquely heartbreaking and revelatory to have an encounter with your former self.

––––––

There is this wall between us, Lord, and it is a wall of mistrust. Please, Lord, tear it down and draw me closer to you.

A "wall of mistrust" with God? Truthfully, I had forgotten I ever felt that way. What changed? How did my perception of God change so dramatically?

In short: not right away, not overtly, and not in any way I could have fathomed. There was no descending of angels or supernatural change of heart. Remarkably and curiously, I see now that God taught me to trust him through the very series of events that I most feared—those "humiliations and painful lessons" I wrote about in my journal. He had not caused them, but he used every last one of them.

I thought about all that had happened between the time I wrote those words and the time I read them again, decades later. In a word, life. Some good things, some really hard things. Disasters of my own making. Disappointment. Distance.

Here's what I figured out from those old journals.

I learned to trust God not because the terrible thing never happened but because it did. I learned to trust God when I failed catastrophically and unmistakably, and he was there. I learned to trust God when I went out into the wilderness, hiding from him and from myself for years (I might have occasionally called or texted), and still, he stood right there waiting for my return.

I realized that the source of my mistrust—my *fear* of the bad circumstances, my *fear* of calamity and doom— was far worse than any actual bad thing that ever happened. Because fear will always leave out one crucial factor: the sweet, saving presence of God himself.

> Fear will always leave out one crucial factor: the sweet, saving presence of God himself.

Fear forgets that God is at hand and working things out for good. No, not necessarily positive outcomes or rosier circumstances. He is not against those things, but that is not the main goal. God, over time, works things out in the direction of closeness to him. His trajectory is of ever-increasing intimacy and communion with him. That's it. Kind of simple, really.

> They will have no fear of bad news; their
> hearts are steadfast, trusting in the LORD.
>
> Psalm 112:7

I learned to trust God
not because the terrible
thing never happened
but because it did.

You never learn anything, not deeply, by just being told. You must be shown.

It took harvesting those old journals to see it, excavating my spiritual past to glimpse God in action. Seeing events over a long passage of time, with the benefit of maturity and perspective, is the closest humans can come to understanding how God must see things. We can see how God works and how he answers a prayer. He is never that far off (Acts 17:27). We choose our steps (and missteps), but he orders our destiny. He watches us, guides us, hears our prayers—but he plays the long game.

It is a great and unfathomable mystery.

It reminds me a bit of chess, which I'm currently relearning after a hiatus of approximately forty years. I had a brief stint in a chess club in sixth grade, but I have long since forgotten the rules and any notion of strategy. My kindergartner is teaching me. He exasperatedly tells me which pieces can move where and what their powers are ("Bishops move diagonally" . . . "Pawns can't attack straight on!" . . . "You're in check, Mom.")

The game is coming back to me, slowly, but for the first few rounds, I routinely lost to my six-year-old. I'd dopily walk right into his trap and find myself checkmated, watching as he gleefully toppled my king. Even a little kid can figure out your most obvious course to victory and will counter your moves at every turn.

Suddenly (finally?), it clicked again. In chess, you need some strategy. You must set up your win multiple moves in advance. You must see a path to victory and start making moves in that direction. You don't guilelessly move in for the quick kill. Your opponent will see it coming. You must be patient and put yourself in position. You must anticipate the other's moves and, in turn, what your moves will be. You must plan multiple moves ahead.

In a way, God is the ultimate chess master. He is an infinite number of moves ahead of us. Yet his goal is not to vanquish. His winning move is the one that brings us closer, ever closer, to him.

———

My journals were a snapshot, an old Polaroid, capturing a split-second moment of my soul and spirit. There was agony and fear, frustration and abandonment. But also hope and truth. And in those gloomy pages, I uncovered a gem. Given all the entries around it, so full of despair, it stands out for its clarity and confidence. Maybe God sometimes does do lightning bolts; maybe he does just come right out and say it. Because here it is, on pen and paper. It just took me a little while, a little more of life, to truly believe it.

The truth is that you love me, you will protect me, you will provide for me and fill the desires of my heart. You alone know what is best for me and the path that I should take. You alone know my heart . . . and know to be gentle with it. You alone delight in me, take joy in me and pride in me. You are my true Father. You would never beat me down, humiliate me, lead me in a false way, or arbitrarily deny me joy and happiness. You forgive me, you bought and paid for me. I am in your family and our bond is blood— unbreakable. You will never forsake me, you will never grow tired of me. You will never change your mind about me, your love is unfailing. You love me because of who you are, not because of who I am or what I have done. You have compassion on me and come to rescue me in times of trouble. You are interested in my well-being and mental health. You care if I am happy or lonely or sad. You watch me, my every move, you breathe every breath with me. I am your precious child; you are fiercely protective of me. You will stand with me and stand up for me, [saying]: "She is mine."

CHAPTER 16

BELIEVING IS BEAUTIFUL (OR, THE SHAPE OF FAITH)

W hy faith?
Why believe at all?
Impossible to answer.
What if we tried it in diagram form?

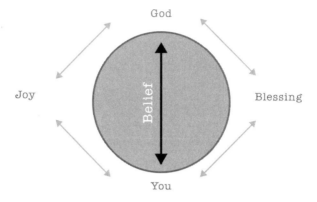

Got it?

Just kidding. You bought a book; let's try words.

Faith. It is clarity and mystery all at once. Answers and questions simultaneously. Satisfaction alongside dissatisfaction, delight alongside despair. Divinity alongside humanity. Nothing pat, pedantic, or perfect, not in this life anyway.

Faith. It is clarity and mystery all at once.

But if it *were* a circle, there'd be God, you, belief, blessing, and joy all intermingling. One divine revolution of interconnected goodness, somehow all working in harmony, in unfathomable order for the benefit of our souls.

Why faith?

Because it is beautiful.

———

I'm sure you've seen those T-shirts or mugs or welcome mats that say "But first, coffee." The trend has really caught on; it's everywhere now. *But first*, yoga. *But first*, pickleball. *But first*, tequila.

If faith were a throw pillow you could buy at Target, the slogan could say "But first, belief."

(Side note to any deep theological types still here: yes, God comes first [John 6:44]. But I'm just speaking from the human perspective because, well, what other perspective can I speak from?)

It's obvious, I suppose. Belief is a precursor to a relationship with God. But in practice, that can cut against all of our human instincts, our impulse toward self-protection in the form of our demands for proof. Especially for us in the modern world, with our core value of "I'll believe it when I see it." With God, it is the opposite. Believing comes first, then we see.

That is how it happened—literally—in the famous New Testament story of the healing of the blind man (Mark 10:46–52). Bartimaeus, a beggar, cried out on the street for Jesus to have mercy on him. His shouts were so loud and disruptive that the crowd shushed him. (Can't you just picture them all congregated in their collective scorn?)

But Jesus came close. "What do you want me to do for you?" he asked.

The blind man replied, "Rabbi, I want to see."

The man's vision appeared immediately.

"Your faith has healed you," Jesus said.

Faith first, then sight.

"What must we do to do the works God requires?"

Jesus answered, "The work of God is this: to believe in the one he has sent."

John 6:28–29

143

I don't know why it is this way. We take a step toward belief, and suddenly, a whole new understanding is revealed. We behold what was hidden moments before. It all starts making sense, emotionally and intellectually. They call it a "leap of faith" for a reason. We must go outside what is safe, known, and provable to step into the divine.

That's what the desperate father in the Gospel of Mark did for his son—taking a chance and bringing his boy to Jesus, asking for him to be healed:

> "[I]f you can do anything, take pity on us and help us."
>
> "'If you can'?" said Jesus. "Everything is possible for one who believes."
>
> Immediately the boy's father exclaimed, "I do believe; help me overcome my unbelief!"
>
> Mark 9:22–24

When we believe—even with our imperfect mix of faith and not faith—a wonderful thing happens. Our spirits have the possibility of flight.

> Though you have not seen him, you love him; and even though you do not see him now, you believe in him and are filled with an inexpressible and glorious joy.
>
> 1 Peter 1:8

I have always loved that phrase: "an inexpressible and glorious joy."

(*Inexpressible*. See? The gospel writers maybe didn't use shapes, but I am not alone in being daunted by this task.)

Divine joy. It's the ecstasy you experience when encountering beauty in this world and feeling a tinge of recognition for its creator. Of course you do. It's someone you know.

I love the changing of the seasons. And not just spring, mind you, though that's clearly the best one, with all the new life springing up, leaves and buds appearing to materialize overnight, the hint of coming warmth. I like all the seasonal shifts. Spring to summer—school's out, schedule's off, and the feel of freedom is fresh and newfound. Then the waning days of summer when you start to sense a crispness in the air, what feels like change and potential in the breeze. Even autumn to dreaded winter carries a certain voltage of possibility. Just when we need a fresh perspective, a nudge out of our ruts, the seasons prod us forward. I see God in the rhythm of nature.

Whether it is the splendor of the natural world, the brilliance of art or music, or an act of human kindness—beauty is God's love language. It is his calling card. We are all designed to respond to it. When you witness beauty, in whatever earthly form it takes, you recognize the author and are filled with that glorious and inexpressible joy.

But the joy of faith isn't just a fleeting, emotional euphoria, a high you might just as well get at a lovely opera or the Taylor Swift Eras tour. It is also an intellectual joy: the excitement and electricity of understanding something new and marvelous, thought-provoking and challenging.

I always think about the story of the two disciples who encountered Jesus as they traveled on the road to Emmaus (Luke 24:13–35). They didn't recognize that the man they were walking with was Jesus until hours later, over supper as he broke bread. Then they marveled. "Were not our hearts burning within us while he talked with us on the road and opened the Scriptures to us?" they asked (v. 32). I love how they said that. Hearts burning within. When our minds and our intellects are pricked and prodded and challenged—this, too, is part of faith's beauty.

———

> Trust in God is deep joy.
> **Pastor Brett Younger, Plymouth Church, Brooklyn**

My newish friend Poppy texted me those words as she walked home from church one Sunday morning. By the way, a friend who surprises you with a quote she heard from her pastor is another kind of joy. Daring vulnerability and deeper conversation with the people you know and discovering spiritual connection there—that is one of faith's gifts.

Whether it is the
splendor of the natural
world, the brilliance of
art or music, or an act of
human kindness—beauty
is God's love language.

While in my forties (and in their eighties and nineties), I made two new friends in former senators Bob and Elizabeth Dole, to my amazement and delight. Mrs. Dole ("Senator Elizabeth," as we call her) asked me to be an ambassador in her campaign to help veteran caregivers. We started working together, doing events and such. But soon, we were more than colleagues; we were friends. And at friendship, the Doles are veterans—experts, really. Calling, emailing, sending books or treats when you least expect it. "I think friendships that share faith are the best kind," she told me when I called to thank her for a devotional she sent. During the pandemic, we even attempted FaceTime with Senators Bob and Elizabeth, their two dogs, and my two toddlers. It was raucous. A few years ago, when Senator Bob passed away at the age of ninety-eight, I had the honor of speaking at the service for him at the World War II Memorial. I recounted his brave and selfless military valor, of course. But I also said this: "Bob Dole taught me it is never too late to make a new friend."

The joy of faith is for the heart, the mind, and the soul. One of God's greatest blessings.

The joy of the LORD is your strength.

Nehemiah 8:10

———

And speaking of blessings . . .
Have a blessed day!
Too blessed to be stressed!
Bless her heart.

Once upon a time, the word *bless* was primarily the sole jurisdiction of salutations for sneezing. Lately, it's crashed into the lexicon. Your barista might tell you to "have a blessed day" as he hands you a latte. A T-shirt might inform you the wearer is "too blessed to be stressed." A proper Southern lady passing judgment on your subpar outfit choice might snicker to her friends, "Bless her heart." (If you've never been on the receiving end of this prettied-up putdown, well, count your blessings.)

We're just blessed all over the place these days!

> "Test me in this," says the LORD Almighty, "and see if I will not throw open the floodgates of heaven and pour out so much blessing that there will not be room enough to store it."
>
> Malachi 3:10

That is a bold promise for God to throw out there. But what do blessings mean in the context of faith? It can't possibly be referring to stuff, material things, worldly prosperity. Surely, it means blessings of a more spiritual nature, right?

Then again, consider the words of Jesus in one of the most well-known passages in the Bible:

> "Blessed are the poor in spirit,
>   for theirs is the kingdom of heaven.
> Blessed are those who mourn,
>   for they will be comforted.

Blessed are the meek,
for they will inherit the earth.
Blessed are those who hunger and thirst for
righteousness,
for they will be filled."

Matthew 5:3–6

The famous Sermon on the Mount goes on from there, but you get the picture. I don't know about you, but despair, mourning, and persecution do not sound like a blessing to me. And asking for a more enjoyable kind of blessing sometimes can feel selfish or indulgent, as though you're hitting up God like some cosmic ATM, hoping he'll churn out some favor.

Recently, I stumbled across a line in a tiny book that had been sitting unread on my shelf for a few decades. It gave me an entirely new perspective:

> To bless in the biblical sense means to ask for or to impart supernatural favor. When we ask for God's blessing, we're not asking for more of what we could get for ourselves. We're crying out for the wonderful, unlimited goodness that only God has the power to know about or give to us.[1]
> **Bruce Wilkinson, *The Prayer of Jabez***

Suddenly I realized that to ask for a blessing means simply asking for more of God. We are blessed when there is more of him in our lives. When you define it that way, those difficult passages of Scripture start to make more sense. Why are you blessed when you are grieving or "poor in spirit"? Because God will be there to the depths of your need. You'll get more of him.

Suddenly I realized that to ask for a blessing means simply asking for more of God.

To ask for God's blessing is not necessarily to ask for a particular outcome (although if you do, of course, he will hear you out!). It means asking God to surge his love to the person, the place, and the circumstance. When I pray to God to bless someone I love, I am asking him to be present and involved—not necessarily to dictate a certain result. If I pray to be blessed at work or at home, I pray he will be with me and bring me more of his divine wisdom, love, and patience. More of him. With me. With you. That's blessing.

> The LORD bless you and keep you;
>   The LORD make his face shine on you and be gracious to you,
>   The LORD turn his face toward you and give you peace.
>
> Numbers 6:24–26

So to review:

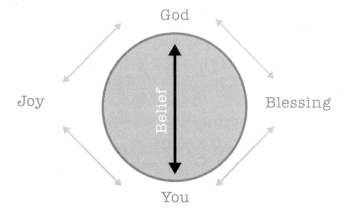

Still no?
How about an Executive Summary:

Believing is beautiful.
God is in the blessing business.
The blessing is God himself.
And that is pure joy.

And the circle is complete.

PART 4

GRACE

CHAPTER 17

DOWN TO
THE RIVER

The quality of mercy is not strained.
It droppeth as the gentle rain from heaven
Upon the place beneath. It is twice blest:
It blesseth him that gives and him that takes.[1]

William Shakespeare

I f you want to make time stop, get in a car and drive somewhere with little kids; a trip that is supposed to be two hours will suddenly feel like ten. Most parents know what to do for a long road trip. Pack games, books, and an iPad if you can. Pack approximately one hundred snacks (and as all grumpy kindergartners will inform you, fruit does *not* count as a "snack"). And pack your inner Yoda because your Zen-like disposition will be sorely tested by the journey.

In New York City, where I live, long car trips sneak up on you unprepared. The best way to describe the traffic is everything, everywhere, all at once. (Or as a driver here once told me, "There's lanes, but nobody cares about lanes.") A trip of fifteen blocks that should take ten minutes can easily take an hour. There you are—no entertainment, no snacks, no way out. Trapped. You gotta keep the conversation lively. I'm big on Would You Rather. Would you rather have ice cream or a milkshake? Hot dog or hamburger? Pool or beach? Beach or mountains? Ski or swim? Soccer or basketball? Basketball or football? Football or . . . no, really, trust me, it's captivating.

Recently, my mom visited and had the misfortune of accompanying us on one of these unplanned forays through city traffic. Mercifully taking the baton from me after my conversation starters began to lull ("Let's rank the days of the week. Tuesday is the worst. Can we agree?"), she told a story about a formative experience she had when she was my kids' ages. Like any good Grandma story, it was part adventure, part morality tale. My mom is eighty-one now, the story more than seven decades old, but my normally boisterous and bouncy children sat enraptured as she recounted with vivid and fresh detail the time she defied her father and nearly lost her life.

The scene unfolds in 1950s Kentucky. My mom, an athletic and adventurous ten-year-old, was on summer vacation with her family. Despite her father's stern, severe, and repeated warnings, she decided to go swimming in the treacherous Ohio River and was swept away. She nearly drowned. I could tell you the rest of the story, but it's better when she does:

I was always told not to swim in the river, but at ten years old I was proud of my swimming abilities (after all, didn't my sister and I swim every day?). On the weekends, my family joined our extended relatives at our camp in Ross, Kentucky, located along the Ohio River.

The camp was little more than a shack on stilts complete with an outhouse. Together with a small contingent of other shacks, we bordered Jake's Amusement Park, which housed two giant swimming pools fed by artesian well water, baseball fields, a few decrepit rides, and an indoor-outdoor café.

My sister Debby and I swam in the frigid pools, sometimes fished with Daddy in the river, begged Cousin Sammy for rides in his speedboat, and generally spied on the grown-ups and explored our surroundings with our friends. Watching the teenagers smoke and drink stolen beer down by the water was one of our favorite things to do. We relished our freedom. My father's one strict admonition: "Do not go in the river."

On this particular day, we found ourselves alone on the dock. Feeling bored and a little rebellious, I told Debby I was going to jump in and swim around a bit, just to feel what it was like. Usually the daredevil of the two, she was horrified at this idea.

The water was calm, so I ignored her pleas and jumped in, calling for her to join me. As she watched, I felt something pull at my legs and then sweep over my entire body as it dragged me quickly down the river away from my screaming sister. It was a rip current, the danger I had been repeatedly warned about.

My heart beat faster than a spastic metronome; gasping for breath, I tried to fight it as it took me under. I saw the shore retreat and felt fear for the first time in my life. I suddenly remembered that to fight an undercurrent was sure death and I should ride it out until it let me go.

What felt like forever was probably only a matter of minutes and I was released. I could see the riverbank but not the dock. Exhausted, flailing, kicking, I finally collapsed on shore, pushing oil-soaked strands of hair out of my eyes and mouth. I scrambled through the sludge, pulling on tree roots and vines, thorny plants slapping at my legs. Praying Daddy wouldn't find out, I finally spotted the dock.

And there he was, standing still, scanning the river. He caught sight of me crawling toward him.

"I'm sorry! I'm sorry!" I sobbed, terrified now to go toward him, sure that I would be whipped or killed, either of which I certainly deserved.

Instead, he threw his arms out wide, stooped low, and folded me into his embrace.

No discussion, no reprimand, no whipping. I was safe. I was alive. I was loved. I was forgiven.

My kids loved the adventure; I was moved by the metaphor. The image of my grandfather, arms outstretched, waiting for his wayward little girl to come home. The picture of mercy. That is how our heavenly Father embraces us.

When we come back, broken and ashamed, God is waiting. It

does not matter where we've been or what we've done. He does not scold or rebuke, demand an account, or exact retribution. He is just overjoyed we are home. Arms stretched wide, the posture of the cross. "I desire mercy, not sacrifice," Jesus said (Matthew 9:13). He waits for us, with love.

And sometimes he doesn't even wait. Perhaps you recall the famous Bible story of the prodigal son. The parable recounts a wealthy father who had two sons. One worked at home diligently, meeting all his obligations and doing everything right. The other defied his father, left home, squandered his inheritance in scandalous living, and found himself destitute, literally sleeping with pigs. Desperate, he resolved to return home to his father and beg for forgiveness, asking for no more than to be treated as one of the hired hands. Precious son—that was a status he knew he no longer deserved. Ashamed and chastened, he set off for home.

> "But while he was still a long way off, his father saw him and was filled with compassion for him; he ran to his son, threw his arms around him and kissed him."
>
> Luke 15:20

While he was still a long way off. God does not wait for perfection before he forgives us. He does not require a changed life before he shows us mercy. His mercy precedes us. He forgives us while we are still a long way off. He meets us, more than halfway. All he asks is that we come.

God does not wait for
perfection before he
forgives us. He does not
require a changed life
before he shows us mercy.
His mercy precedes us.

_____

CHAPTER 18

THOU CHANGEST NOT

Great is Thy faithfulness, O God my Father;
There is no shadow of turning with Thee;
Thou changest not, Thy compassions, they fail not;
As Thou hast been, Thou forever wilt be.[1]

"Great Is Thy Faithfulness"

Ah, how I love the old hymns.

Church music has massively upped its game since the old days when it was a reliably clomping piano, staid choir, and, on special occasions, an organ. (My mom and I once confessed to each other's delight that neither of us can stand the organ.

Our little secret. Don't tell anyone!) These days, at many churches, Sunday services feature full-on "praise and worship" jam sessions with multipiece bands, including drums (!). These contemporary songs sound as good as anything you might hear on the radio—except the main focus in the lyrics is Jesus instead of "my baby." If you happen to be in Manhattan some Sunday, come visit the church I attend, Good Shepherd New York, and you'll hear some of the finest musicians anywhere.

Still, the songs that resonate most deeply within me are the classics from the old hymnbook that I can still see set right next to the Bible in every church pew. "How Great Thou Art." "Fairest Lord Jesus." "It Is Well with My Soul." I can't say I appreciated these songs all that much as a kid. Their words were formal and hard to understand; the performance in my 1980s Baptist church didn't exactly set hearts ablaze. I remember how I would settle into the wooden seats, quickly scanning the service leaflet to see which hymns were selected, looking for the hoped-for words: "stanzas 1 and 4 only." Yay! The shorter the hymn, the quicker the post-church visit to Dunkin'.

Yet somehow these hymns managed to burrow a place deep in my soul, a kind of buried treasure lying dormant for me to discover years later. I now regard the lyrics I once considered stodgy and impenetrable as poetic and inspired, a kind of bonus holy text. These hymns are a soundtrack to my faith, the musical accompaniment to some of my most distinct spiritual memories: "Just as I Am" playing every week as the pastor issued an "invitation" for people to come forward and accept Christ as their Lord and Savior. "Holy, Holy, Holy"—my father's favorite hymn, for its joyous and buoyant tone. (Now, whenever I hear it at church, I imagine it is a wink from him from beyond. Or perhaps a message from God telling me: *Your dad says hi!*) And I will never forget my mother planning the music for my father's funeral, insisting on peppy, upbeat hymns for the service. "No dirges," she said. Even in shock and grief, she wanted the music to reflect our belief that we would one day see him again. Her determination and grit were (and are) a marvel.

> I now regard the lyrics I once considered stodgy and impenetrable as poetic and inspired, a kind of bonus holy text.

But standing alone among all of these memories and associations are three words: "Thou changest not." I guess it's because they are the words I always need to hear.

God does not change. His opinion of us does not change. His love for us does not change. "As Thou hast been, Thou forever wilt be," as the lyrics of the great hymn go on to say.[2]

This is not how my brain works.

My internal dialogue can be merciless; my self-assessment is like a stock rising and falling, scrolling across my psyche like a CNBC ticker across the bottom of the screen. *Kindness was down today sharply, while gossip and pettiness were on the rise. Patience soared early but plummeted in the afternoon hours. Self-recrimination hit historic highs.*

God might not change, but I changest a lot.

A colleague of mine once observed: "It's like firing yourself every night, then rehiring yourself in the morning."

Exhausting.

I suppose this hypervigilance derives from childhood, growing up with my highly changeable father who lit up the room, but whose moods could change and darken unpredictably. I trained myself to sense the atmosphere, always sussing out the emotional ambiance to adjust myself accordingly. I tried to be a good girl—at least on the surface—to avoid calamity. For most of my life, I have been a textbook people-pleaser and peacemaker.

And those qualities easily transferred to my relationship with God. It was not hard to imagine that internal voice of reproach belonging to him. When that happens—when judgment is constant but compassion is nonexistent—despair is inevitable. And—if you've mistakenly attributed your self-scolding voice to God—it creates a distance from the very one you need most.

> When judgment is constant but compassion is nonexistent— despair is inevitable.

It is a hard habit to break. But with the grace of advancing age, these childhood behavior patterns have softened as I've become older and a bit wiser. The little girl who always wanted to please and keep things calm is learning to live through the discomfort of people not always being happy. I'm slowly learning to accept I cannot try to set and maintain the emotional temperature of the room at a perfect seventy-two degrees.

And my relationship with God has changed the more I have learned about him and experienced life with him, dialing in to his love and grace.

God does not change.
His opinion of us does
not change. His love
for us does not change.

> It is for freedom that Christ has set us free.
>
> Galatians 5:1

I once found this verse so odd: repetitive and unnecessary. But then I started to love it. It's so emphatic—almost like God is saying, "Duh!" Christ didn't come and set us free so we could imprison ourselves. He did it so we would actually be free.

So let's *be* free then!

Free from our own self-assessment. Free from comparison to others. Free, even, from the well-meaning judgment of our families and coworkers and friends. Being open-minded and receptive to the areas in which you need change is one thing. But it is another to berate yourself relentlessly, imagining you're obtaining some spiritual feat by the rigor of your self-flagellation.

> Without faith it is impossible to please God.
>
> Hebrews 11:6

These are the words every lifelong pleaser needs to hear. Not long ago, I discovered an old journal entry where I retranslated this verse, addressing it to myself: *Stop thinking you have to earn it or arrive at some spiritual nirvana,* I wrote. *All you have to do is believe.*

God wishes us freedom from self-assessment.

God alone is the judge of our souls, and he promises compassion. God alone is the author and perfecter of our faith (Hebrews

12:2), and through his love, mercy, and truth, we are quietly transformed. Let's breathe that in. Real internal change does not come at the point of a weapon or the threat of

God alone is the judge of our souls, and he promises compassion.

eternal damnation. It comes upon glimpsing, and then absorbing, the wholly unmerited and extravagantly generous expression of his astonishing grace.

That love, we can be sure, "changest not."

Being confident of this, that he who began a good work in you will carry it on to completion until the day of Christ Jesus.

Philippians 1:6

CHAPTER 19

SIN AND LOATHING

M y friends and I went through a shoplifting phase when I was in junior high. I'm not proud to admit this, even all these years later. But it happened. We would rendezvous at the supermarket, standing around the parking lot, working up the nerve. Then one at a time, we filed in, casually sauntering around the beauty aisle, sliding a mascara or lipstick into our purse or pocket. There was the thrill and the terror, the shot of adrenaline, and then: a massive hangover of guilt for me. Long nights of tossing and torment and promises to God to never, ever, ever do it again . . . until the next convening of the preteen posse and the inevitable pull of peer pressure.

I regret to say this happened more than once and more than twice; it went on for a good part of a summer until one night, the guilt was so overwhelming that I confessed to my mother. I will never forget the look of grim disgust on her face. "Go back to your room," she said, "and bring me every single thing you stole. Every. Single. Thing." It was mortifying to return with the haul— far more than she likely imagined—eyeshadow, Lip Smackers, Tic Tacs, eyeliner, all splayed on the back porch table. But as painful as it was to confess to her, I felt a singular relief. She was disappointed, I was punished, but she still loved me. I found freedom in telling the truth—to come clean meant the burden could be lifted. And there was a certain simplicity to it—the wrong was clear, the guilt appropriate, and the reprieve was not withheld.

I grew up in a traditional Baptist church where guilt and sin, heaven and hell were major preoccupations. Perhaps love, mercy, and forgiveness were also on the menu, but they certainly weren't the main course. I constantly felt my own sin, my fundamental and immutable character flaws. I often had a gnawing but vague sense of guilt or "being in trouble"—a feeling of dread that continues to this day.

Back then, at church or sometimes even at home, it was common for a grown-up to say, "The Holy Spirit must be convicting you." That word—*convict*—was as heavy as a set of bricks laid upon my heart. And as a child, I don't think I even grasped its full meaning. Now I know. Convict is what the legal system does to criminals. The law applied, the sentence determined, and the punishment executed. Considering it now, I find using that word astonishing in the context of faith. Of course, the Bible speaks of Jesus returning to convict the world (John 16:8), but it also says he came to save the world, not to condemn it (John 3:17). My religious upbringing emphasized the former far more than the latter. Heavy on guilt, light on grace. No wonder I grew up fearing God more than loving him. To me, to know God was to be judged by God, and to be found wanting, of course.

My father had a deep sense of personal shame. Sometimes he would sit on the back porch, the weight of his sin almost visible on his drooping shoulders. A darkness could surround him like an inky, despondent shadow. Those were the times when it was usually better to avoid him. But sometimes, he was talkative—voluble in his stream of (guilty) consciousness. He spoke about his dark side, the bad Charley. Nothing specific—he was far too decent a man to unburden himself on a little girl. But to hear him say such things even in vague terms, my heart ached. "Oh, Daddy, don't say that," I might offer. "You aren't bad!" But he would shake his head as if to say, "If only you knew. You don't really know me."

My father's exacting self-reflection was deeply affecting, and, as it turns out, contagious. It was not hard to imagine his rigorous self-scrutiny applied to me; it was not hard to model the behavior. I developed a practice of constantly scanning for my own sin, ever vigilant.

> Heavy on guilt, light on grace. No wonder I grew up fearing God more than loving him.

My father's own harsh self-judgment also came to represent God's judgment to me. It is exceedingly easy, especially as a child, to conflate our earthly father with our heavenly Father. I felt I needed to identify every wrong, confess it, ask for forgiveness, and God forbid I miss one—or worse, self-justify or let myself off the hook—then, my salvation itself was in jeopardy. Sure, there was forgiveness—that was why Jesus died on the cross, of course!—but only after proper repentance. That just invited new ways to fall short. Was my repenting satisfactory? Was I sorry I did that bad thing or was I sorry because I was supposed to be sorry . . . but not really sorry, and God would certainly detect the deception? Double trouble.

I wondered if my very faith was sufficient. I spent years of my formative preteens wondering and worrying, *Does God think I'm a Christian? I think I am. I think I believe, but does God believe my belief? And if he doesn't, am I damned to the eternal fire?* My spirituality was a never-ending cycle of self-assessment, blame, and fear. It was heavy.

No wonder so many have left church, left faith, left God. It is a wonder that I didn't . . . that I didn't just say, "To hell with it," (literally). Only a miracle, only God himself could have saved me from that version of "salvation."

Many people have had this version of religious experience. Many have understandably run from an unforgiving, fire-and-brimstone orthodoxy. But in some ways, the pendulum

> Only a miracle, only God himself could have saved me from that version of "salvation."

It is exceedingly
easy, especially as a
child, to conflate our
earthly father with our
heavenly Father.

now seems to have swung dramatically in the other direction: no guilt, no shame. No love or mercy either. To speak of guilt, sin, or wrong is cringeworthy, backward thinking, an embarrassing relic of a bygone era, as garish as big hair and shoulder pads.

We reassure ourselves with affirmations, with inspirational quotes, with declarations of our worthiness and enough-ness. It's a flattering Instagram filter applied to our souls. Briefly satisfying but ultimately unconvincing—and no match for the truth we deeply sense about ourselves. And somehow, at the same time, our modern times feel more unforgiving than ever. One strike and you're out. Delete your account; delete your life. Grace and redemption are ever more vanishingly rare.

What do we do when we do wrong, and we know it? Where do we take the metaphorical pile of drugstore makeup and spill it out on the table? What do we do with shame? Does it have any place in a healthy sense of self?

I know one thing. If we can't confront the truth about ourselves—what's good and what just isn't—then we are likely to avoid ourselves, distract ourselves, anesthetize ourselves. We will run from ourselves into work, sex, drugs . . . or even positive things like exercise or wellness routines taken to unhealthy levels. (I once heard a pastor say that sin is "when a good thing becomes an ultimate thing.") Our shame cycle is on high spin: avoid, distract, self-loathe, repeat.

To quote the apostle Paul, "What a wretched man I am! Who will rescue me from this body that is subject to death?" (Romans 7:24).

Cue big-faced, blow-dried television preacher: "Friend, you need the Lord!"

Eh. I prefer how Eugene Peterson put it: "The only accurate

way to understand ourselves is by what God is and by what he does for us" (Romans 12:3 MSG). In other words, something amazing happens when we tell the truth to God, believing he hears us and removes our wrongs from us. We don't have to run from ourselves. We don't have to hate ourselves.

———

I've been thinking about all of this when it comes to parenting. Let's face it: kids can be awful. They're human nature in raw form. They lie. Like, a lot. They hit and pull and bite. They can be self-centered and unappreciative. Kids tell tired, barely-holding-it-together moms, "I hate you." Kids ask Alexa, "Who is the meanest person in the world?" and expect the answer to be "Mommy." (Well, my kid did that once.)

I don't want to repeat the shame-torment of my childhood. But I don't think my kids will be served by a "you can do no wrong" wheel of affirmation—not when they're confronted by real life and their real humanity, which will never be perfect and blameless. It wouldn't be right to send them into the world unequipped with tools to handle their disappointments—including disappointment with themselves.

My daughter is particularly sensitive, deep, and introspective. She is a wise, empathetic, and beautiful little soul. She is my angel. But, of course, she is no angel. Like any child, she is prone to a fit of temper or meltdown over some perceived injustice or privilege denied. Most times, it comes and goes. But sometimes, she has a moment of self-reflection. She might say, "I know I'm acting selfish," or "I'm just a brat. Admit it."

Sometimes this is for dramatic effect, and sometimes it's genuine remorse. It's not for me to figure out. I tell her this: "If you feel in your heart you did something wrong, tell the truth to yourself, and tell the truth to God. Then it's over. God washes it clean. For God, it's like your sin never happened. You might find it hard to forget what you did wrong. You might even try to remind him, 'But remember that awful thing I did?' And God will say, 'No, I don't. I don't know what you're talking about. You're forgiven and the slate is clear.'"

This works for adults too.

When my own shame and dread cycle returned to me recently, when I was berating myself over some failure, a word of perspective came to me—so striking I wrote it in my journal:

If I have sins to answer for, I answer to you, not to me.

I answer to the Lord, who is "compassionate and gracious, slow to anger, abounding in love" (Psalm 103:8).

There is no greater feeling than confronting and facing your weaknesses and shortcomings, and finding out that you are loved, accepted, and forgiven anyway. It is better than telling yourself you're perfect or good enough or at least better than [insert much more terrible other person]. And it is much, much better than your self-condemnation, the merciless beatdowns applied to yourself.

We can be honest with ourselves about who we are, because of who he is. The one who sets us free. God is here. So we are free.

Where the Spirit of the Lord is, there is freedom.

2 Corinthians 3:17

CHAPTER 20

HE RECLINED

A few years ago, I went through a spiritually trying time. Actually, that is a disappointingly bland way to put it. Let me try again. A few years ago, I was certain I was being cursed by God or possibly haunted by a demon.

It happened during the years I was a law student in Washington, DC. I was under a tremendous amount of stress and pressure, no question. Yet it was surprising because it happened when I felt very close to God. I was doing a Bible study every day. I was praying faithfully. I felt connected to my spiritual side in a visceral and deeply meaningful way.

All of a sudden, guilt started to overwhelm me. A crushing,

damning, accusing guilt. I was obsessed with my own sin. I couldn't shake the thought. It harassed me day and night. I tormented myself, excavating every corner of my life and conscience, looking for my failings and flaws. Even confessing to God, which normally brought relief, was of no help. I confessed and confessed but found no peace.

I had nightmares—visions that felt terrifyingly real. Sometimes I awoke in bed feeling a dark presence hovering over me. I could even hear it breathe—literally, the sound of nostrils flaring. I knew something was there, but I was too terrified to look, to come face-to-face with this ghastly presence. I just squeezed myself tighter into a fetal position, buried myself in my covers, and prayed. Bible verses I had memorized. The lyrics to hymns I knew. Just the word *Jesus.* Anything to find relief. Eventually, the darkness would flee and sleep returned.

After this went on for a miserable while, in desperation, I called the pastor of a church I had attended in Arizona years prior. I don't think he even remembered me, but he was kind enough to take my call. I explained to him that I was overcome by a sense of my own sin. I told him God or the Holy Spirit must be condemning me, that I had prayed for forgiveness repeatedly, but the feeling would not leave.

What he said next changed my thinking and my life.

"You have to ask yourself something," he said. "What exactly is your concept of God here?"

It forced me to reckon with myself. What was this version of God I was imagining? Certainly not the God I had ever known. The one I loved and who loved me. The God I had been conjuring was a God of damnation, accusation, condemnation. It was a God with no mercy.

At times, we might imagine God's voice in that way. A voice that indicts us. A voice that accuses. A voice that reads us the riot act for our sins. This is dangerous territory, indeed, but not for the reasons you might think. If we feel shamed, threatened, or alienated, we may start avoiding God, closing our ears, creating distance. That is the opposite of what God is trying to accomplish with us. This is what my period of torment taught me: my self-berating was not God's voice. In fact, it was a counterfeit voice.

This is not to say that God only communicates shallow assurances and platitudes. Our God is not a God of happy talk. On the contrary, God is quite good at confronting, cajoling, challenging, and persuading. But when he does, it is entirely consistent with his loving and kind nature.

> When evening came, Jesus was reclining at the table with the Twelve. And while they were eating, he said, "Truly I tell you, one of you will betray me." They were very sad and began to say to him one after the other, "Surely you don't mean me, Lord?"
>
> Matthew 26:20–22

The scene of the Last Supper always strikes me. Jesus was reclining when he predicted his betrayal and death. *Reclining.* You have to be careful not to read too much into something like that, to overanalyze. (I've learned on the internet that a dinner repose was the common practice of the era.) But his physical posture at the Last Supper somehow matched his spiritual posture. He was not confrontational or overly emotional. He spoke from an intimate, relational position. Yes, his words had authority and were devastating. He pulled no punches. Yet he didn't browbeat or inflame.

Our God is a firm and straightforward truth teller.

I once read an article that fascinated me: "Why I Gave Up Drinking," by Sarah Bessey.[1] In it, she described a journey in which she felt called to give up her social drinking. She didn't quit because she had a drinking problem per se. It was just something she increasingly felt on her heart. What caught my eye was how she put it: "I quit drinking because I felt like God asked me to quit drinking."

Obviously, my first thought was, *I sure hope God never asks me to do that.*

But the wording she chose stood out to me. God didn't command or accuse—he asked. Sarah called God's voice "gentle but relentless."[2]

> In my life, when it comes to the dawning of change, it can feel as if God presses a thumb down on something in my life. As if to say, "*here*, this spot, this one, let's stay here for a while. I want to lean on this."[3]
>
> **Sarah Bessey, "Why I Gave Up Drinking"**

God is completely in character, even at the difficult moments. God remains kind and loving even when talking to us about an area of our lives that needs to change.

———

At my church, we do a corporate confession. We read these words together:

> Most merciful God, we confess that we have sinned against you in thought, word, and deed, by what we have done and what we have left undone. We confess that we have not loved you with our whole hearts. We have not loved our neighbors as ourselves. We humbly repent. For the sake of your son, Jesus Christ, have mercy on us and forgive us, so that we may walk in your ways and delight in your will to the glory of God the Father.

Churches worldwide say some version of this prayer at Sunday service. It can be a drag, this confession business. It can be rote recitation. Or it can be a great relief. It is a moment loaded with opportunity.

Our pastor, Michael Rudzena, makes the most of it. He suggests we quietly reflect, asking God for a holy memory, something to come to mind that we may need to take responsibility for. We sit in silence. And then he ministers with words of comfort. He often says that confession is not meant to be a "cosmic beatdown" or an occasion for "morbid introspection." It is simply being accountable for the ways in which we fall short of love.

We then close with this beautiful scripture: "As far as the east is from the west, so far has he removed our transgressions from us" (Psalm 103:12). Or as Eugene Peterson translated it: "As far as sunrise is from sunset" (MSG).

God doesn't just forgive our failings and then let the memory of them hang around, tormenting us. He takes our guilt far away and replaces it with his peace.

That day back in law school, after I spoke to the pastor, my season of feeling cursed and ashamed began drawing to an end. It didn't happen all at once, but over time. And I had to retrain my thinking. When those feelings of guilt and accusation would begin to rise, I reminded myself of who God is: my rescuer and my friend. I went back to basics. Sometimes all the way back, reciting to myself the sweet, familiar words of the children's hymn: "Jesus loves me, this I know."

> **"In repentance and rest is your salvation."**
>
> Isaiah 30:15

This is what I learned. Salvation has two parts, not one.

Repent, then rest.

Rest in the knowledge that you are loved and forgiven and embraced.

Recline.

God doesn't just forgive
our failings and then let
the memory of them hang
around, tormenting us. He
takes our guilt far away and
replaces it with his peace.

CHAPTER 21

MERCY ME

In a fit of humiliation and rage, he killed him.

About thirty years ago, I saw a scene in a movie called *The Mission* that I have never forgotten. The film is loosely based on a true story about a group of Jesuit missionaries in colonial South America in the late 1700s who came to convert the indigenous people to Catholicism. (It pulls no punches about the fraught nature of that effort or the brutality of the time period.) I recently rewatched it to see if the scene I had remembered so vividly held up. It did.

The movie tells of a native people, living in a magnificent yet unforgiving mountain region high above the waterfalls—almost beyond outside reach. Almost. Robert De Niro plays a mercenary and slave trader named Rodrigo Mendoza. The first time we see Rodrigo he is capturing native adults and children—in a net—to sell them into slavery. He is unrepentantly vicious and arrogant, a fearsome and feared man cutting a reign of terror in the community. That is, until one day he returns home to find that his lover has left him for another man. That's when, in a fit of humiliation and rage, Rodrigo kills him.

The man is his own brother, whom he dearly loved.

Rodrigo descends into despair. The law provides no punishment for his "crime of passion," so when we see him next, he is in a prison of his own making. Living in squalor, shackled by his own guilt, lying in torment, wishing for death.

A priest, played by Jeremy Irons, pays a visit, but Rodrigo has no time for a man of God. "For me, there is no redemption," he tells him.[1] The priest challenges him to accept penance, a way to pay for his sins. "There is no penance hard enough for me," he replies.[2] And yet crushed by shame and eager to suffer, he agrees.

———

The penance calls for Rodrigo to return to the mountain, back to the villages he once ravaged—this time making the grueling and unforgiving journey with an enormous makeshift pack strapped to him, a homemade beast of burden—metal, wood, and rubbish bound together by rope and tethered to his back. His expiation is to haul it up the mountain, the same one he once traversed on his mission to capture slaves. Day after excruciating day, he struggles to tow his cargo to the peak, navigating treacherous falls and scaling cliffs by his fingernails—his load, heavy as a millstone, pulling him ever downward. When he is near collapse at one point, some of the younger priests in the traveling party rush toward him to cut the pack loose. He refuses. He has not paid his penance. He will not permit himself to be relieved of his burden.

It culminates in one of the most powerful depictions of forgiveness I have ever witnessed. A scene with no words spoken.

Exhausted and near death, the rope now strapped around his neck, he arrives at the top of the mountain, where he comes face-to-face with the indigenous people he once trapped and sold like chattel. The little ones see him first and recognize him immediately. They know exactly who it is.

The leader of the people approaches and pulls out a knife. Rodrigo is certain he is about to die—and surely, that is what he deserves. The man places the weapon to his neck, holding it there. Rodrigo awaits his execution. The knife is lifted and brought down violently—but only to sever the rope and unleash the pack, the wretched load sent spiraling down the cliffs to the river below. The burden is gone. The weight is released. The priest, watching the scene unfold, rushes in, kneels, and wraps his arms around Rodrigo, rocking him like a baby, tears of deliverance rushing down his cheeks like waterfalls.

Deserving of death, given life. Redeemed at the hands of the very ones he persecuted.

Is there any more transformational force in the universe? Is there anything more powerful to effect change within the human heart? Whether or not we realize it, many of us are walking around with our shame strapped to our necks like a hunk of junk, strangling us, holding us down. But God severs it for good. All we must do is stand still before him.

> When we understand forgiveness, flowing from the work of Jesus and the Spirit, as the strange, powerful thing that it really is, we begin to realize that God's forgiveness of us, and our forgiveness of others, is the knife that cuts the rope by which sin, anger, fear, recrimination and death are still attached to us. Evil will have nothing to say at the last, because the victory of the cross will be fully implemented.[3]
>
> **N. T. Wright, *Evil and the Justice of God***

God hacks off our burden and our shame, frees us, then envelops us in love. The failings we are afraid to admit, the sides of ourselves we would never dare show, the sins within that even we cannot forgive—they go tumbling down the mountainside.

The spontaneous response to this overwhelming gift of grace is deep relief, gratitude, and loyalty. If there is a fast track to closeness with God, his mercy is it.

God hacks off our
burden and our
shame, frees us, then
envelops us in love.

> I love the LORD, for he heard my voice;
> he heard my cry for mercy.
> Because he turned his ear to me,
> I will call on him as long as I live.

Psalm 116:1–2

For a long time, I thought these verses meant we are to call on God for the rest of our lives out of a sense of debt, a requirement to pay back his favor. But I read it differently now. I see that receiving God's grace is the ultimate bonding experience with him. It connects us to him eternally with a cord of our choosing—not a rope or shackle but a link, a tie, an attachment. We will tug on that line again and again. We will need his mercy over and over. We will indeed call on him all the days of our lives—out of choice and out of love.

If there is a fast track to closeness with God, his mercy is it.

We need not pay a penance for our own sin—it is already paid. God loves and forgives us not because our contrition is profuse or because we brutally self-flagellate. He offers grace for free.

Our mission is to say yes.

> He has saved us and called us to a holy life—not because of anything we have done but because of his own purpose and grace.

2 Timothy 1:9

PART 5

HOPE

CHAPTER 22

JESUS
ANSWERED

My husband and I have a recurring joke. In the typical scenario, it goes something like this: I walk into the bedroom at night with a glass of water. "Oh," he will remark, faux-perturbed. "Did you get me one?"

"Shoot, I'm sorry!" I'll reply, faux-abashed. "Want me to go back and get you one?"

"Nah," he says. "I'd rather have the issue."

We get a big kick out of this routine. It's funny because it's honest. Sometimes we'd all rather have the issue than the resolution.

We'd rather have the one-up, the few extra bucks in our emotional piggy bank (usually to spend the next time we're in the wrong). We don't want the problem fixed or the wrong righted. We want the issue.

It can be like that with God. We'd rather have the doubt than the faith. We'd rather have the questions than the answers.

> "You will seek me and find me when you seek me with all your heart."
>
> Jeremiah 29:13

In the Gospels, we encounter two words again and again: *Jesus answered.* Walking that dusty path toward his destiny, he often responded to questions. Many people approached. Some genuinely sought him. Some tried to outsmart him or set a trap. Others were a mix, convinced their questions were earnest only to have his answers penetrate their veneers. Yet none of that determined whether Jesus responded.

Questions are not sacrilege. Apathy and disinterest are far more grievous offenses. Here's what I believe. Come as you are. God answers. Just be sure to come.

———

When grappling with doubt, a good first question is the one we pose to ourselves. *Am I earnestly asking? Or am I erecting obstacles to God for some other reason? Am I genuinely seeking information and understanding? Or am I trying to create distance? Are my questions a pretext to avoid intimacy and vulnerability?*

I say this not because God will answer only when our hearts achieve some exalted state of super-piety. God does not withhold his presence and perspective until we present him with a pure, inquiring heart. But when our motives are a mess, we may find it harder to find him. We may find it harder to hear him. Or we may find him but feel that what we receive is unsatisfying or that we heard nothing at all—because our actual question is something else entirely.

In my daughter's classroom, the teacher has a placard displayed: "Temporary Uncertainty Is Encouraged." What's true for third graders is true for us: being momentarily unsure is the gateway to understanding. An authentic relationship with God invites uncertainty and questioning.

Everyone trying to walk a spiritual path in this flawed world at some point grapples with doubt. If you never have, perhaps you haven't thought about it hard enough. Or maybe you feel you have been fortunate to be blessed with a great, unwavering faith. And perhaps you have!

But doubt is not a lack of faith. It is not the opposite of faith. It is an aspect of faith—a feature, not a bug, as the computer nerds like to say. Doubt is just faith being worked out, like a muscle. Put in the effort, do the reps, and ask the questions—it's spiritual strength you're building.

The famous cliché when you start law school is that

An authentic relationship with God invites uncertainty and questioning.

your books and professors teach you "how to think." Not what to think but how to analyze facts, assess arguments, present evidence. You learn rather quickly that you can never ignore the problems in your own position. If you are making an argument, of course you present your best evidence. But you also address the counterarguments. You engage the evidence arrayed against you. If you ignore it, your position will be exposed as weak; you will not be nearly as persuasive. And when your opponents get the chance to stand up, they will let you have it.

God is ready to address the counterarguments. He doesn't ask for blind faith. He doesn't ask us to set aside our intellect to believe in him. On the contrary, he sparks our intelligence, teases it out, and challenges our thinking. God yearns to engage in these matters.

In the Gospels, Jesus appeared to his disciples after his death and resurrection. In Luke's version, upon seeing him, the disciples were described as "startled" and "frightened" (Luke 24:37). They thought they had seen a ghost. Jesus asked, "Why do doubts rise in your minds?" (v. 38). He detected their doubt and responded. *Look at my hands and my feet. Ghosts don't have flesh and bone, but I do.* "Touch me and see," he told them (v. 39).

I have always wondered what I would have done in that situation. Walk up and touch his hands and feet? Or hang back, afraid to approach, to go out on a limb? I'll never know. But here is what I do know. In the face of our doubt and fear, Jesus says, in effect, "Come closer." He does not recoil or take offense. To him, our skepticism and questioning are an opportunity for deeper connection. So often our instinct is to do the opposite, to keep our distance.

Doubt is just faith being
worked out, like a muscle.
Put in the effort, do
the reps, and ask the
questions—it's spiritual
strength you're building.

_____

God yearns to engage in these matters. So bring your questions to God. Bring your bright mind, bring your intellect. But also, bring your stout heart and your strong legs because, in the end, there will always be a leap. A leap of faith.

Not every doubt can be assuaged as easily as the touching of a scarred hand; not every question is immediately and decisively answered. Especially not the big, existential ones, such as "Why is there so much evil in the world, seemingly unchecked?"

Whole volumes have been written, even an entire branch of religious studies—Christian apologetics—devoted to addressing such matters. (FYI, that is so not this book.) I don't know if any answer could ever be sufficient, not in this life, not while we are still flesh and bone, "[seeing] through a glass, darkly" (1 Corinthians 13:12 KJV). Not when we are actually feeling, experiencing, and engaging with real suffering. Even if there were some cosmic, catchall explanation, it would likely seem esoteric and antiseptic. Removed from and irrelevant to the real world.

Why does God allow suffering?

Why would a loving God allow evil in the world to persist?

Why does injustice go unchecked, millennia after millennia?

Why doesn't God swoop down and put an end to it, once and for all?

I have wondered these things aloud to God.

Sometimes this is what I hear back.

It is not over yet.

Evil will not prevail.

I did swoop down.

I broke off a piece of myself and came into the world to change everything.

I am doing it.

You want me to crush evil in one decisive blow, but that would crush humanity itself.

The world you know would end.

I am on a different path, a redemption mission.

Demonstration instead of destruction.

Showing, not forcing.

Love, not violence.

This takes time.

I'm not done yet.

It would not be hard to find the flaws in reasoning or leaps in logic, but for the moment, this makes sense to me. Or at least, it brings me some peace. I am willing to believe.

> Faith simply invites us to coexist with the doubt and belief within us—to live with our questions and live with God.

When we work out our questions in the presence of God, answers may not be possible, but relationship can be. Faith simply invites us to coexist with the doubt and belief within us—to live with our questions and live with God, simultaneously, as opposed to all alone with one or the other.

Reason is on our side, love.[1]
Bono

CHAPTER 23

THE OVERNIGHT
NOTE

You know how all the wellness experts say you should never look at your phone right before bedtime? And you should never sleep with your device on your nightstand? And you should never, ever, ever look at your phone very first thing in the morning?

Yeah. I'm so failing at wellness. Give me an F-minus. I fall asleep reading my iPad most nights. My phone is my alarm clock (actually, I should say "alarms clock" since I set several). And pretty much the first thing I do in the morning—after I make my coffee—is look at the dozens of new emails on my phone in order to get ready for work that day.

And there it sits, like a ghoulish grim reaper haunting my inbox. The Overnight Note.

The *TODAY Show* broadcasts four hours a day, but it is a twenty-four-hour operation. Producers work quite literally around the clock to get the show on the air. As soon as the show ends in the morning, everyone starts working on the next day's rundown. And because it's a morning news show, some of the most crucial work happens when most folks are asleep, including me.

That's when the indispensable and highly caffeinated staff on the graveyard shift prepares a nightly report that encapsulates every major headline nationally and internationally from the previous twenty-four hours. Not all of this will go into the show, of course. But the note informs the anchors and senior producers of most major news events worldwide so we are "read in"—up to date on what's happening—and can make judgment calls about which stories should be added to that day's broadcast.

Unimaginatively, we call it the Overnight Note. On most days, it is a staggeringly depressing document.

U.S. Surpasses 400 Mass Shootings So Far In Calendar Year
Investigators Probing Serial Killer On Long Island
Woman Found Dead In National Park After "Apparent Bear Encounter"
8 Injured In Lake Boat Crash, Driver Charged With Boating While Intoxicated

Coast Guard Searching For 4 In Capsized Boat Off Gulf Coast
3 Seriously Injured When Small Plane Crashes In Residential
  Neighborhood
Firefighter Dies After "Targeted Attack" On Fire Station
25 Hospitalized After Deck Collapses At Country Club
4 Killed In Helicopter Crash In Remote Alaskan Lake
Woman In Wheelchair Hit And Killed By SUV
June Hottest Month Ever Recorded On Planet Earth: Weather
  Service
Greek Authorities Evacuate 19,000 People As Wildfire Blazes
Russian Missile Strikes On Odesa Kill 1 And Damage Historic
  Cathedral
3 Dead In Washington State Listeria Cluster
Children's Cups Sold Online Recalled Over Newly Detected
  Lead Levels
Watching TV As A Kid Linked To High Blood Pressure And
  Obesity As An Adult: Study

That's just a sample. That is just one day. (And I spared you the political headlines.) On and on it goes, story after depressing story. You can't possibly click on them all, nor would you want to (*Toddler Dies After Mother Accidentally Locks Her In Hot Car*). This is a snapshot of our world—and my morning wake-up call. Sometimes it feels like taking twenty punches to the gut in rapid succession.

This is part of the job, and I am not complaining. To host *TODAY* is pretty much otherwise all joy. I'm surrounded by people I adore who are at the top of their professions; the work we do is meaningful and challenging. We also laugh—a lot. Every day I wake up feeling among the luckiest people on earth—yes, even when that first alarm goes off at 3:00 a.m.

But these days, we all get some version of the Overnight Note. Whether we turn on the news or are bombarded by social media, everyone can relate to that feeling of being overwhelmed by everything that is wrong in the world. All the heartache. All the torment. All the division. All the rage. It can feel like death to our spirits by a thousand cuts—a thousand tiny pinpricks to our hearts. We look down and find we're bleeding and don't know why. We feel deeply wounded in our souls.

We need hope. We need faith. But how do we find faith in a world where the Overnight Note could easily be ten pages instead of five? How can we truly find hope and faith in the face of so much awfulness?

And what about these convictions we hold—what if they are sadly misplaced? What if there is no coming justice? What if this really is all there is for the world, and then it ends? Arbitrary suffering with no hope of eternity. Nothing transcendent, no silver lining. Just humanity's ever-devolving race to the bottom, earth's ever-forward march toward ruin. What if this whole idea of God is just a figment, a soothing story we tell ourselves? A fever dream, a sweet salve of delusion?

To that, I say, yes, please. Butter me up—I'd like to soak in that salve.

———

Most of us, at some point, will wonder if what we believe just simply isn't true. I certainly have. I've let myself entertain the possibility

Everyone can relate to that
feeling of being overwhelmed
by everything that is wrong
in the world. It can feel like
death to our spirits by a
thousand cuts—a thousand
tiny pinpricks to our hearts.

that this is all there is, that our notion of redemption and eternal life is just a fiction, something I learned as child and grew emotionally attached to. There is no heaven and there is no God.

But at some point, I decided that I didn't care. It didn't really matter whether I got to the end of my life, died, and realized it was all a lie, that I had been wrong all along. I still preferred to spend my life believing.

This is what it comes down to for me: I would rather be hopeful and wrong—than hopeless and right.

I would rather spend my life in a state of believing, a state of optimism and expectancy—even if I am someday proven to be a fool. Because believing that the world is irredeemable—and plenty is out there to vindicate that position—is no better option. Being correct that the world is lost provides no comfort. It does not make life more bearable. Cynicism and despair only pile more heartbreak upon the original heartbreak. Hopelessness does not solve the problem; it compounds it.

> Hopelessness does not solve the problem; it compounds it.

Every one of us is forced to grapple with evil and suffering. Our modern world and its relentless, never-ending news cycle do not allow us to hide or deny its presence. We all must make sense of it. Do we do that alone, with despair and resignation? Or do we make sense of it with God, and with hope?

In his book *Evil and the Justice of God*, N. T. Wright wrote:

> We are not told—or not in any way that satisfies our puzzled questioning—how and why there is radical evil within God's

wonderful, beautiful and essentially good creation. One day I think we shall find out, but I believe we are incapable of understanding it at the moment, in the same way that a baby in the womb would lack the categories to think about the outside world. What we are promised, however, is that God will make a world in which all shall be well, and all manner of things shall be well, a world in which forgiveness is one of the foundation stones and reconciliation is the cement which holds everything together.[1]

I do believe that one day the rights will be wronged, the broken will be made whole, the unloved will be fully loved, and we will all be fully known. That promise acknowledges our real pain here and our future hope: "And hope does not disappoint, because the love of God has been poured out within our hearts through the Holy Spirit who was given to us" (Romans 5:5 NASB).

> I heard a loud shout from the throne, saying, "Look, God's home is now among his people! He will live with them, and they will be his people. God himself will be with them. He will wipe every tear from their eyes, and there will be no more death or sorrow or crying or pain. All these things are gone forever."
>
> Revelation 21:3–4 NLT

In the end, in this life anyway, we cannot know if our faith is correct or if it is sadly misplaced. But we can believe. And I have

I do believe that one day the rights will be wronged, the broken will be made whole, the unloved will be fully loved, and we will all be fully known. concluded that believing is, at the very least, a better way to live.

This isn't a one-time decision that we never have to revisit. We choose hope, live out our day, go to sleep, wake up, and choose to hope again. The choice is ours. With every sunrise. From the moment that alarm goes off.

Because of the LORD's great love we are not consumed,
for his compassions never fail.
They are new every morning.

Lamentations 3:22–23

CHAPTER 24

AN ACT OF GOD

My lovely friend sat across from me. We sat by the fireplace, cozy with blankets, our kids somewhere in the basement—entertaining each other or perhaps burning down the house. Honestly, as long as they left us alone for a precious few, we didn't care. We were content, cradling our coffee and absorbed in our conversation.

I had known Laura (not her real name!) for a little while. She was a close friend of one of my dear friends, so we had been thrown together many times, immediately clicking in social settings. But this was the first time we had ever spent a long stretch together, just us. We bonded, shared our stories, made the kind of deep, soulful connections that we girls are so good at. (In law school, my roommate Meridith and I used to meet on the couch every Sunday morning to have a heart-to-heart and a good old cry over coffee. We called these sessions "Tissues and Issues"—or "T&I" for short.)

Now it was Laura and I doing "T&I." We talked about what got us through some of the hardest moments in our lives. She had just been through a particularly dark period. She had lost a pregnancy at twenty weeks, then nearly lost her life from a related infection. The pain of losing her baby was crushing; in the hospital, she cradled her little girl's tiny body, wrapped in a blanket, and said goodbye. Losing a child and her own near-death ordeal was traumatic enough. But there was more. She later learned that she had been the victim of poor medical advice and, ultimately, a careless doctor. Trauma upon trauma, grief upon grief—the dawning realization of being lied to and manipulated by her caregivers shattered her last vestige of resilience. She descended into a place of deep despair, sick in body, sick at heart. She sought help everywhere, in every acupuncturist, empath, therapist, intuitive healer, guru—she was desperate for relief. As her older kids went off to school, she sat alone with no vitality except for the obsessive (her word) energy to find something—anything—that would return her to herself.

As we sat by the fire, she had come a long way from that dark place. She had done the work, and then some. A year prior she had attended a retreat that unlocked profound change within her. She came to believe that, in some ways, she was her own healer; the power was within her all along, as the Good Witch in *The Wizard of Oz* told Dorothy. The fruit of her work was evident. She had a new way of living and new practices to center her. She gave up drinking (not so much because she had a problem, she explained, but because she felt so darn good in her new perspective and didn't want anything to alter it!). She gained a deep inner confidence, trusted herself more, maintained boundaries, and gained strength. She was a changed person—yes, even better than before.

As we sat together that day, she was thoughtful and introspective. She said, "Maybe God had those things happen because I needed to go through this journey." Perhaps, she reasoned, this was the way to discover this better way of life and better path she was now confidently on.

The words struck me and touched me. This is so often the wisdom we cling to, the sense we try to make out of our suffering. Gamely, we make valiant efforts to find some meaning in pain, some silver lining in the blackest of storms. For those of us of faith, we often make God a character in this narrative. "Everything happens for a reason," people are fond of saying. "God was teaching you a lesson!" or "God won't give you more than you can handle." And the very worst of the genre: "God must have needed another angel!" when someone dies far too soon. We even refer to natural disasters—a tornado or earthquake or hurricane—as "an act of God." As if God were some great meteorologist in the sky arbitrarily raining down calamity upon the earth.

No.

No, no, and no.

The more I understand and know God, the more I have a visceral reaction to this, even though I have sought refuge in these kinds of sentiments many times in my life and found a certain comfort there. I tried to make sense of my father's death that way. My father was a deeply complicated and tormented man. Perhaps God saved him from a life of continued struggle and inner disappointment by taking him as a young man. An even more audacious thought: perhaps his untimely passing, which shattered our family, was ultimately an act of compassion on us as well. Because though we adored him, he could be mercurial and terrifying, his severity and judgment deeply influential. Perhaps his passing was the only way the rest of us—Mom, Cam, Annie, and I—could be free to flourish as our true selves. My father would have almost certainly disapproved of my two career choices—television news (Shallow! Phony!) and the law (So many lawyers already!). It is a testament to our human resilience when we try to see painful life events in this way. And sometimes these things can contain some truth as well.

But I cannot believe that God is the author of evil. The Bible says God is "good to all; he has compassion on all he has made" (Psalm 145:8–9). I take him at his word. We cannot simultaneously believe in a loving God and believe that the same God would cause suffering in some calculated effort to teach even the most essential of lessons. We should aim higher for God and have a higher opinion of him. God is God. He has plenty of angels and can teach lessons and course correct without exacting inordinate and undeserved suffering on his children.

———

This is important, because thinking otherwise, even if we conclude that our pain was "all for the good" in the end, makes some peace with our suffering and some peace with God. But I worry it is a surface peace only. What could remain—in a place we may not even dare go—is fear and resentment of God. You might be too good-hearted or devout to give voice to these thoughts or even let their whisper cross your consciousness. I have a rebellious and irreverent streak. I am prone to think, *Okay, God, really? Was there really no other way to accomplish your goal here? I can recognize and even be grateful for some other positive outcome, but was it really necessary to put me through the wringer to achieve it? And even if I am convinced you had no other option, where does that leave me now? How can I trust you, God, if I fear you may be devising another misfortune for my next painful life lesson?*

If our belief structure, whether consciously or unconsciously, includes a version of God exacting pain on us, it is potentially problematic. At a minimum, it creates a trust problem with God. Our guards will be up; a distance will be created. I just have to believe this is always the opposite of God's goal. Everything we can glean from the Scriptures and the life of Christ demonstrates God's fervent desire for closeness to us.

But perhaps there is a grain of truth to seeing God's hand, even in anguish. Perhaps the true answer is not all that far off. God doesn't cause pain, but he does turn our pain into promise. He turns suffering into meaning. He turns weeping into dancing. Redemption from seemingly impossible circumstances is, in fact, his specialty.

I am reminded of Joseph's story in the Old Testament. His jealous brothers sold him into slavery in Egypt. They assumed he was long dead. But Joseph forgave his brothers and told them, "You intended to harm me, but God intended it for good" (Genesis 50:20).

It is a great comfort when our perspectives are broadened, when we see the events of our lives in a bigger picture, a better light, a God's-eye view that makes sense of even the most unimaginable sadness in our lives. God does not cause evil and suffering. But he can transform it. It is a phenomenally fine distinction, but one that matters.

We live in a broken world. A world of accidents, unfairness, and sickness. A world of plane crashes and child abuse. A world of lying and manipulation and shallowness. A world that sometimes seems set up for the wicked to prosper (Job 21:7).

This is not the world God intended or one that he will allow to persist forever. But while we are here, while he is working out a cosmic rescue and reconciliation that is far beyond our understanding, he promises to be present with us. He promises to make good out of bad. He promises to transform what is wrong into something that is right.

That *is* an act of God.

God doesn't cause pain,
but he does turn our
pain into promise. He
turns suffering into
meaning. He turns
weeping into dancing.

CHAPTER 25

WHAT ABOUT JOB?

Heaven, we have a problem.

I have a hard time believing God outright causes evil and suffering. It isn't consistent with the God I know. But at the same time, we face an excruciating and undeniable fact. Sometimes, he allows it. And if he allows suffering—when he could stop it—what's the difference? It might as well be him causing it.

I don't like this truth, but I cannot run from it or sugarcoat it. If we really believe in an all-powerful God, one with supernatural sovereignty over time and space, then we must believe he possesses the power to protect us and shield us from harm—and sometimes doesn't use it.

Why?

This is the ultimate "Why, God?" for me—the ultimate threat to my faith. I can imagine no greater challenge to our belief than when something devastating happens to us or, even worse, someone we love.

A few years ago, *60 Minutes* did a profile of parents who lost children in the Sandy Hook massacre. The story featured an array of families and the different ways they coped with the unimaginable. At the end of the piece, a woman named Nelba Márquez-Greene appeared. A compact, curly-haired, bright-eyed young mother, she lost her six-year-old daughter, Ana Grace, that day. Perhaps you remember images of the angelic little girl with the curls like her mother, sitting with her brother at the piano, enthusiastically accompanying him as he played "Come, Thou Almighty King."

The Márquez-Greenes are a family of deep faith. *And what of that faith now?* the interviewer asked her. *How do you hold on to belief in the face of such loss?*

I will never forget her response. I have shared her words with others over the years and, to this day, cannot utter them without a sob rising up in my throat. Nelba replied, "The moment I'm reunited with her, I want to hear two things. I want to hear, 'Well done, my good and faithful servant.' And I want to hear, 'Hi, Mom!'"[1]

How to reconcile unmerited suffering with belief in God? Nelba's words show the way. Faith does not and cannot explain why the innocent are allowed to suffer. It simply gives us hope that there is a place and time when that suffering will end, when connections will be restored, when life will be eternal—"On earth as it is in heaven" (Matthew 6:10).

Years later, I met with Nelba. Her words and her example had nestled into my heart. I couldn't shake her from my mind . . . and I didn't want to. Finally, I worked up the courage to invite her to lunch. I wanted to understand more about her faith and grief—how she made sense of the senseless. We met at a winery not far from her house. She brought salads, slices of almond cake, and a copy of the sermon the pastor had given at Ana Grace's memorial service. She was warm and open and generous of spirit. Her very existence is a triumph of good over evil.

Nelba told me that six months before the shooting, she and her husband had attended a Bible study at their home church in Winnipeg, Canada, where they had long resided. Nelba was born in Puerto Rico; she and her husband, Jimmy, both grew up in Connecticut. Only months before the massacre, they had moved back to the Northeast, to a new town called Newtown, ironically, dreaming of finding a safer and quieter place for their children to grow up than they had ever known.

Their Bible study centered on Job—to me, one of the most disconcerting and disturbing books of the Bible. As the story goes, Job was a devout and faithful man whom God permitted to be tested greatly. Job lost everything: his wealth, his position in the community, his friends, his family. Yet he held on to his belief in God, defying Satan's predictions that people remain faithful only when blessed, that they abandon faith at the first sign of suffering.

Faith does not and cannot
explain why the innocent
are allowed to suffer. It
simply gives us hope that
there is a place and time
when that suffering will end.

Job remained committed, and in the end, having proven his devotion, God blessed him—restoring to him everything lost—wealth, position, power, even a new family.

I have never liked this story. Even if God "made good" on all that Job lost, who wants a replacement family? How are you supposed to recover when God permitted you to go through such suffering? How are you supposed to trust him ever again?

Nelba sees things differently. And if she can, then surely, I can too. Surely, I must. Nelba believes God gave her that study of Job to prepare her for what was to come. So that on the day of their despair, she and her husband would be equipped with "a robust and gutsy faith." *A robust, gutsy, rugged faith.* Those were the words used by Nelba's pastor in the moving and powerful sermon he had given at Ana Grace's memorial service. The one whose copy she brought to our lunch.

She shared with me an extraordinary story about one of her darkest hours. Sometime after Ana's murder, with her sadness and despair overwhelming, Nelba prayed a prayer of desperation: "I will do anything at all, even give my soul to Satan, for just one more moment with my little girl." She fell into a deep sleep and had a profound dream. I would call it more like an Old Testament vision. She dreamed that she had Ana again, but there was no God. It was a dark and unbearable reality. When she awoke, she was changed. She knew this lonely and broken road she was forced to walk, this grieving life she now inhabited, would remain one of faith. Gutsy, robust, rugged faith.

When my father died, I remember some of my friends asking whether I could still believe in God, whether his sudden death at the age of forty-nine had made me doubt my beliefs. "No," I said.

"This is when I need God most." Nelba said something similar. She never considered deserting her faith; she never considered abandoning God. But she said, "I do have a lot of questions for him."

That's the answer. There is no answer. Sometimes faith is simply choosing to live, choosing to coexist with questions for which there will never be a satisfying explanation. Not in this life anyway.

Someone once asked the renowned pastor Tim Keller why a good God would permit unmerited suffering. He responded that any answer he gave would be like a bucket filled only three-quarters of the way.[2] It is a mystery. We don't know. God doesn't give us those answers. He just gives us himself.

> "In the same way,
>   you are now in anguish,
>   but I will see you again,
>   and your hearts will rejoice,
>   and no one shall deprive you of your joy.
>   On that day,
>   you will not ask me anything further."
>
> John 16:22–23 NCB

On that day, we won't have any more questions. We will have understanding, and more importantly, we will have him. We will have life; we will have eternity. We will have our dear ones restored to us. No more weeping, no more agony, no more mourning. Heaven is the world God always intended.

CHAPTER 26

SEND ME HOME

I'm thankful for the time God has given me, but I'm ready
to see Jesus. I can't wait to see Jesus. Send me home.[1]

Timothy J. Keller

O f all the words I could imagine uttering on my deathbed,
I'm not sure I could ever muster those. I love God and I
truly believe his promises of a better eternity, but when
push comes to shove, that is still a giant leap. No one lives to tell
what happens next (by definition). When I'm staring death in the
face, I'm not sure I will have the calm and astonishingly hopeful
and expectant disposition of Timothy Keller.

Keller was a pastor and teacher I greatly admire. For years, I
attended his church, Redeemer Presbyterian, in New York City. He
died at seventy-two after a long struggle with cancer. I remember

when I used to think people in their seventies were old. I don't think so anymore. He was too young.

Timothy Keller ("Dr. K" as my close friend and frequent churchmate Lindsay and I nicknamed him) had an enormous influence on my understanding of God. He was a preacher so gifted that the church he founded in the heart of New York City—not exactly considered a religious mecca—grew to four locations. On Sunday mornings, he shuttled from service to service around the city, arriving after the service began to deliver the sermon, then departing out the back door when finished to get to the next one. He couldn't be in four places at once, so on any given Sunday, you were never sure when he would be at your location. If you tried to call ahead to find out which service he would preach, the church receptionist wouldn't tell you, lest no one come to the others. So you'd roll the dice and go to the service that suited you, hoping you'd win the lottery that week. Your heart would lift when you saw him walk in quietly during the hymns. It made church like a secret speakeasy where Bono was doing a surprise acoustic set. In that way, it was quintessentially Manhattan, where vying for a good table or hot tickets is a way of life.

Many people told me to check out Redeemer when I moved to New York City. The first time I went, I didn't understand what the fuss was about. His delivery was unassuming, his appearance ordinary. The church service was staid and dry—the old hymns were pounded out on the piano, and the teaching text, archaic and impenetrable, dutifully read. Then Tim stood to speak. Out came pouring a brilliant exposition of biblical teachings that was somehow both scholarly and emotional. Your heart and your mind came alive. The feeling was reminiscent of the two disciples on the way to Emmaus: "Were not our hearts burning within us while he talked with us on the road and opened the Scriptures to us?" (Luke 24:32).

Hearts burned when Tim preached the Word. He had a gift of making archaic teachings come alive, his observations brilliant and moving, peppered with his subtle humor. He was prone to declarative statements, pithy and penetrating, such as "You are simultaneously more sinful and flawed than you ever dared believe, yet more loved and accepted than you ever dared hope."[2]

I never knew Tim personally, never got to meet him. But his teaching introduced me to God in a way I had never contemplated before. Even after I moved away and stopped attending Redeemer, I still bought his books, listened to his sermons online, and followed him on Twitter. That's how, in May 2023, I saw his son's tweet that Tim was in the final stages of his life and had been moved to hospice care. His time was near. "His family is very sad because we all wanted more time," his son Michael wrote.[3] But as for Tim, he just wanted to see Jesus.

I can't wait to see Jesus.

Note the word choice. Not *meet* Jesus—*see* him. Tim was not afraid of where he was going because he knew someone there. He was going to see Jesus, not meet him for the first time.

When I think about death and dying, when fear rises, this thought comforts me. Of all that is unknown about what comes next—Where will I be? What is it like? What do you do there all day?—what is known is Jesus. It's kind of like when you dread going to a party or work event because it's going to be full of strangers. It only becomes bearable if you find out that you will know at least one person there. In the case of the afterlife, the only comfort I have is that I will be greeted not by a stranger but by a friend.

Jesus is our link between this world and the next. He is there and he has been here. Sometimes I think about his arms outstretched on the cross. I imagine one hand reaching into the next world and one hand reaching back to ours. He is the connection. He is the way we can hold hands with eternity.

Jesus is our link between this world and the next.

Sometimes this gives me great comfort. And sometimes I'm still afraid.

> When they saw him, they worshiped him; but some doubted.
>
> Matthew 28:17

The disciples believed, but they doubted. Belief and unbelief both in one short sentence. Does anything better encapsulate what it's like to be human? We see just a portion of what God is doing, not the whole picture. Death is the greatest of unknowns. Of course, we are afraid. Of course, we question. We believe, yes—and we doubt. God is okay with both. God knows and understands.

On his deathbed, Tim told his son, "There is no downside to me leaving—none."[4] I love his certainty. I love his declarative sentences—pithy and penetrating—right to the end. I aspire to that faith and certainty and expectant hope. Tim was my teacher until his dying breath, though we never met. Not yet, anyway. I can't wait to see him.

PART 6

PURPOSE

CHAPTER 27

THE
FRAGRANCE OF
THE GOSPEL

W hen I was in church as a young teenager, the youth groups were always on us to tell our friends about Christ, to "witness" to others about our faith. (*Witness* used as a verb this way! An affront to grammar as well as to delicate teenage psyches.) This was quite literally the last thing I wanted to do. For most of my adolescence, I wanted to blend in and disappear. I wanted nothing to distinguish me in any way, shape, or form from every other human in my teen orbit. I hated my curly hair. I hated my chubby frame. I didn't even like my name. It was so different, especially back then. Savannah? You'd never find it on those little license-plate key chains you begged your mom to buy at the grocery store. Why couldn't I have been Bridget or Denise or Jenny? Everything that made me different was a source of deep humiliation.

For example, I was (inexplicably) deeply embarrassed that the handlebars of the new bike my parents had scraped and saved to buy me for Christmas looked different from my friends' bikes. Their handlebars were curved; mine were straight across. Too much difference for me to deal with. Thus, I rarely rode the bike, to my parents' bafflement and dismay. It sat in the garage, shiny and barely touched—a source of embarrassment to me at school and a source of guilt and shame at home, knowing I had hurt my parents by so cavalierly disregarding a gift they had worked hard to make a reality.

So when the youth pastor told us we were to tell our friends about Jesus so they could be "saved," it was a big "No thank you" from me. Even well into college and early adulthood, I wasn't exactly up-front about faith or religion. I didn't hide it, but I wasn't looking to introduce the subject into conversation. (My life was certainly no model of moral rectitude, either—yep, that was me at the sorority party carrying a personal six-pack of beer around!) I found journal entries from my late twenties and early thirties where I scolded myself for not being more forward about my faith. I confessed in those pages that even my dearest friends had no idea how important my faith was to me. God was a dirty little secret I carried.

Making matters worse, I certainly didn't want to be in the company of those I saw proclaiming their Christianity loud and proud. The ones who showed up to protests with big placards saying "God hates [insert group X]." God hates? Huh? To quote Bon Jovi, "You Give Love a Bad Name."[1]

And yet.

And yet, and yet, and yet.

That is no excuse not to share the good news of God. In fact, it is all the more reason to get the word out. Loud and proud.

Here's the thing. If you found a spray that miraculously zapped red wine stains off your white couch, you would tell everybody, right? Why? Because it's great news and you'd want all your friends to be in the know.

That, to me, is the spirit of evangelism. That's what we are to do. Tell people the good news that God loves them so they can get in on it. God will take care of the rest.

But thanks be to God, who in Christ always leads us in triumphal procession, and through us spreads the fragrance of the knowledge of him everywhere.

2 Corinthians 2:14 ESV

I have always been struck by that word: *fragrance*. Notice it doesn't say *smell*, or *odor*, and certainly not *stench*. It isn't like one of those ladies in church wearing too much perfume. *Fragrance* evokes

Tell people the
good news that
God loves them so
they can get in on
it. God will take
care of the rest.

something lovely and pleasing and, above all, gentle. God told us how to do it, right in those words.

Jesus Christ didn't force himself on anyone. He didn't needlessly harangue. He answered questions. He told stories. He firmly and plainly spoke the truth. And when rejected, he didn't protest or resist. In fact, he let himself be put to death. His "witness" was his life. His testimony used precious few words.

> Preach the gospel at all times.
> When necessary, use words.[2]
> **Attributed to St. Francis of Assisi**

Scholars disagree on the exact wording of this quote, its meaning, and even whether St. Francis said it. (In fact, the theologian who reviewed this manuscript told me modern experts no longer think it's St. Francis!) (Hi, Joel!) That's fun for scholars, but for the rest of us, the gist is clear: share the good news you know about God, not just with your words but also with your life, your character, your core.

This is carrying the fragrance of God, something only possible, by the way, when we are near him. The more we keep company with God, the more that aroma lingers—of love and acceptance, gentleness and forgiveness, truth and authentic peace. We don't have to force it. Just be in God's presence and his essence becomes part of us. And when we are far from him, yes, the fragrance wears off.

I remember the gospel story when Mary washed Jesus' feet with

> Share the good news you know about God, not just with your words but also with your life, your character, your core.

expensive perfume. The scripture says, "The house was filled with the fragrance of the perfume" (John 12:3). In my imagination, the fragrance was the love and gratitude she felt from being in the tender presence of God.

Those around Mary protested that wasting that pricey perfume was indulgent, when it could have been sold for charity. Did they genuinely want to help the poor, or did they want to lord it over Mary? The gospel doesn't say. Except this: Jesus stuck up for Mary and told everyone, essentially, to let it go. *Let this fragrance be spilled, let the aroma rise up and fill this space. Heartache and sadness and need will always be with us. We need love and kindness and goodness to fill the air too.*

Follow God's example, therefore, as dearly loved children, and walk in the way of love, just as Christ loved us and gave himself up for us as a fragrant offering and sacrifice to God.

Ephesians 5:1–2

This book began with that verse: the one from Ephesians that once seemed stuffy and distant to me. The one translated to "mostly what God does is love you." The one that changed my outlook on faith.

And lo and behold, right there in the original, something new for me to discover.

Fragrant.

I must have read this verse a thousand times, yet I just saw it for the very first time. God really does speak our language.

We don't need bullhorns and bumper stickers. We don't need to accost people on the street. We don't need to grammatically mistreat the word *witness*. May we all simply exude the sweet aroma that is a telltale sign of time spent with God: goodness, kindness, and love. And let that fragrance linger in the air.

CHAPTER 28

MOSTLY WHAT
WE (CAN) DO

The image woke me up out of a dead sleep. Strange, because I barely even noticed it the last time it flickered across my screen—perhaps numb from seeing it so many times before. The commercial is on regular rotation during the daytime hours of cable news that flash continuously on the walls of my workplace, where television monitors are mounted on every available space like wallpaper. It's an ad for a charity in Africa called Mercy Ships that offers free medical procedures aboard a cruise-sized vessel to people with desperate, disfiguring, and—if they had had the fortune to live somewhere else—easily curable or preventable diseases.

Their conditions are shocking and devastating: facial tumors enlarged grotesquely to the size of baseballs, children beset by advanced cleft palates. These are the images that woke me in the middle of the night. I thought of all of those people, walking around in pain, in deformity, ostracized by a culture that understands their condition as a sign they are cursed, that they have somehow offended God. They live in the shadows, barely treated as humans.

This was the thought that jolted me out of sleep: *How does that person feel that "mostly what God does" is love them?* A flush of shame washed over me. What a Western, privileged, obtuse view of spirituality.

Why must people suffer? Worse: Why must some people suffer while others flourish? This is the question, doubt's mic-drop moment. The crucible of faith.

Answer? There is no answer. No good ones at least. It makes no sense. It is not right. It is not fair. I don't know how people expect to feel loved and cherished by God when their earthly experiences are almost entirely made up of suffering. These questions are so disturbing and distressing, the proffered explanations so unsatisfying, that I fully understand why they are often a fatal stumbling block to faith, an insurmountable obstacle to belief in God.

Okay.

But.

Our valid spiritual questions should be no obstacle to doing what we can do about it.

Mostly what we can do is love them.

I believe that is what we are divinely called to do.

How does anyone who suffers unfairly feel that "mostly what God does" is love them? When they feel that love from us.

For those suffering, God might be too difficult to believe in, too far removed, too esoteric a concept to be felt. Who can blame them? But love, care, and touch from a fellow human being, right alongside them, should not be. When we look someone in the eye, offer our coat, or invite a stranger to sit with us, we transmit the love of God. Whether the recipient recognizes it is not the point. God is not needy or neurotic, looking for credit. He seeks his people, all his people, to feel loved and cared for and cherished. He is glorified when his children are the deliverers of that love.

How does anyone who suffers unfairly feel that "mostly what God does" is love them? When they feel that love from us.

Here is the amazing thing. In this immense and unfinished work, God invites us to participate. You. Me. Us. God pays human beings the ultimate compliment by drafting us into his Great Commission. He deputizes us as his agents—to spread the love that we see in him everywhere.

New York City is full of type-A people. I confess to being one of them. Sometimes at work, I might grumble to myself, "I am just going to do this research myself, rewrite this script, or make this call personally . . . because it is just easier." It's the old "If you want anything done right, you gotta do it yourself" mindset.

Ever hear that phrase? Ever say it to yourself? (Guilty!) It's the ultimate put-down to others, isn't it? It's saying, in effect, "You're not good enough to help with this. You won't do it right. This one is too hard, too big, too complicated for you." It is a lack of faith, a vote of no confidence—the withholding of a chance for others to shine, to surprise you, to learn, to blossom.

This is not God's way. He says the opposite. He says, *Come with me . . . I will show you how to do what I do. I will show you how to love people into completeness.*

Ponder that for a moment. This is the God of the universe believing we are worthy and capable. When he invites us into this work, he gives humanity a high honor, the ultimate dignity. He gives us a mission and meaning.

More than wealth, more than fame, more than knowledge or wisdom, more than beauty, more than praise—that is what we crave. Purpose. God gives us a profound, divine purpose—love each other—and invites everyone to be a part of it. Jesus always viewed us as his plan A.

———

Not long ago, I witnessed a sadly familiar sight in New York City: an unhoused man holding a sign that asked for food. The scene caught my eye more than usual because he had two young children with him, also holding signs. I was walking to an after-school program with my daughter, who was about the same age as the kids on

When he invites
us into this
work, he gives
humanity a
high honor, the
ultimate dignity.

the street. I thought about how different our children's lives were—this stranger's and mine—and how fundamentally unfair that is. A pang of guilt overtook me. Running late, as usual, I kept walking and dropped off Vale, hoping she hadn't noticed or absorbed the scene.

On the way back, I resolved to pass the family again and ask if I could buy them dinner. When I arrived, someone had beaten me to it. The kids were happily noshing on a fresh pizza. But I noticed that the father wasn't eating. "Hi," I said. "Can I get you something else to eat? There is a Subway right across the street. I could get you a sandwich."

His response surprised me. "There is a place that sells lamb right down there," he said, pointing to the next block.

Okaaaayyy, I thought, taken aback. I was a bit put off that he had requested a specific cuisine. *I guess beggars can be choosers,* my snarky side quipped internally. Immediately ashamed, I gave myself the inner scolding I deserved, and we walked together to the gyro place. I bought food and water for the family and went on my way.

If you think I'm telling this story to congratulate myself for an act of charity, think again. On my walk home, I had a poignant revelation. *What would Jesus have done?* I'm pretty sure a lot more than buy a sandwich and walk away. He would have bought the meal, then sat down and dined with them. He would have asked the man his story and queried what else the family needed. He would have exchanged numbers and kept in touch.

The kind of love Jesus calls us to does not dabble or keep its distance; it

His is an all-consuming love.

does not dip in from time to time. It plunges deeply and invests intently. It's the way he loves us, after all. His is an all-consuming love.

Look, we are human. We cannot attain the level of unconditional love that God maintains for all his children. This isn't meant to be a guilt trip. It's an aspiration. It's a hope. It's a calling. It's a belief in your possibility. You don't get a penalty for failing to live up to that level of love; the only failing is failing to try.

Loving strangers is hard. Exposing ourselves and being vulnerable is frightening—even with friends and family. Left to our instincts, most of us can't muster it and don't even want to. We are often too busy, too preoccupied, too wrapped up in our own real struggles. But filled with the love that God has shown us—and choosing to soak in it!—we find ourselves with love in abundance to share. A love like that fills us with joy that is hard to contain within. Divinely aided by God himself, we find ourselves able to do far more than we ever thought possible. He shows us the way.

———

On the Mercy Ships, the doctors say healing begins before even one medicine is administered, before one surgical incision is made. Healing begins at the clinic door, when someone says hello, greets them, shakes their hand, looks them in the eye, and looks past their disfigurement, as if to say, *I know you're in there. I see you.*

We are so tempted to avert our eyes from the suffering all around us. And it is heartbreakingly understandable to think, *I'm sorry, I can't look at you.* To that sentiment, the nurse on the Mercy Ship responded through tears, "People have been telling them that their whole lives. Someone has to look at them; someone has to look them in the eye and tell them, 'You're human and I recognize that in you.'"

When we feel we can't do it—we can't bear to come close to suffering and imperfection and pain—imagine where we would be if God took that approach with us. He never does. He looks past what is disfiguring about us: our self-absorption, our pettiness, our greed, our deception. He looks past our failings and sees our souls. He sees our hearts and who he designed us to be. He pours out his love in abundance.

And that is mostly what we can try to do too.

> The LORD . . . has compassion on all he has made.
>
> Psalm 145:9

He looks past our failings
and sees our souls. He sees
our hearts and who he
designed us to be. He pours
out his love in abundance.

CHAPTER 29

COMMENCING

Every once in a while, I am invited to give the commencement address to college graduates. Not only is it a privilege, but the universities usually give out an honorary degree to boot! (I don't know what you're supposed to do with an honorary degree, but I figure it's like shoes—you can never really have too many?) When asked, I usually say yes, and then . . . immediately wish I hadn't. It is so intimidating to figure out a compelling, meaningful, relevant message to deliver to people on the brink of starting their adult lives. What did you want to hear from your graduation speaker? Do you even remember who spoke at your graduation? Exactly. I just imagine those poor graduates, robed captives in unfortunate headwear, hungover and baking under the late spring sun, dreaming of a "hair of the dog" Bloody Mary at brunch, wishing their speaker—*Who is this person again?*—would just wrap . . . it . . . up.

Or maybe that was just me.

On the other hand, speaking to the next generation is also an incredible opportunity to pause and take stock of your life, zoom out on your experience, and harvest what you've learned. My dear friend and *TODAY* colleague Hoda Kotb loves to listen to commencement speeches for inspiration in her downtime (while the rest of us slobs relax with *The Real Housewives*). She says the best speakers give "everything they've got." They take all the experience and knowledge they have accumulated over a lifetime and put it out there—like turning your pockets inside out to find every last piece of change. You're wringing out your life to squeeze out every drop of wisdom.

I truly feel for young adults just starting out their lives and careers. They're on the precipice, their whole lives in front of them; they have so much to look forward to. But they also have that charged emotional stew of uncertainty, hope, fear, and ambition. I never understood middle-aged adults who romanticize youth. I mean, sure, I'd take an unwrinkled face (and anything approaching abs), but I wouldn't wish the worries of youth on my worst enemy. I remember my own angst-addled mindset: *Will I ever meet the right person and have a family? Will I ever get out of this town and make something of myself?* Something like ambition burned within me, but I was insecure, afraid, and occasionally inert, not knowing where to begin.

So when I stand at the dais on commencement day, I imagine talking to myself among the crowd, the twenty-one-year-old me—the one with the high hopes and the high hair. What do I wish I could have told her?

Something like this.

Do you know how many times you will "ruin your life" or "ruin your career"? Quite a few. Oops, you did it again.

But God is not daunted. He can handle a few of your missteps.

In fact, given the chance, he will dazzle you with how he can weave your mistakes into something surprising and beautiful.

When people sometimes ask me how I "got here," I have to smile. It was not a straight line. It was a zigzagging, dotted, sometimes broken line, with pauses and detours and disasters. Beginnings that ended too soon. Endings that turned out to be beginnings.

The beginning is a good place to start—all the way back to my very first job in television news. Nothing about me screamed, "Future *TODAY* host!" In fact, I was fired from my first job two weeks after I started.

I had just graduated with my journalism degree from the University of Arizona and tried to land a job in television news. It wasn't easy. There were precious few on-air jobs, and it was the classic situation. The job listings all wanted someone with on-camera experience. But how do you get on-air experience if you can't get hired without it? I needed a break; I needed someone to give me that first chance. But truth be told, I wouldn't have hired me. I was objectively terrible. My voice sounded like a squeaky little girl's, and my hair— let's not even talk about my hair. But after months of searching and sending out résumé tapes all across the country, I landed a job in the

God is not daunted.

He can handle a few

of your missteps.

tiny town of Butte, Montana—one of the smallest TV markets in the country. They hired me sight unseen for the tidy sum of $13,000 a year. I joined a newsroom staff of four (including me). I was lucky to get that job—and thrilled! I just knew I was on my way. My friends threw me a big going-away party. "You're going to be the next Joan Lunden!" they enthusiastically told me.

I set out from my hometown in Arizona—the first time I had ever lived away from home. My father died right before my senior year of high school, and my sister and I both went to the local university. We couldn't afford the dorm, so we lived at home. And anyway, we both felt we needed to keep my mother company. Moving to Butte, Montana, after graduation was a life milestone as well as a career one.

I packed up my car for the two-day drive. My mom came with me and helped me find my first apartment, a tiny one-bedroom in a building that seemingly hadn't been touched since Butte's mining boom in the late 1800s. I remember the joy of going to Walmart with my mom to buy stuff to set up my apartment. I can still see the four-piece dish set with the little blue and yellow flowers she bought me (in fact, I still have one of the mugs). I was excited to start my life. My own apartment, a new town, a real job. I showed up on the first day of work, red-blazered and raring to go. *Butte, Montana, I have arrived.*

Ten days later, they closed the station. Seriously. It was over. Don't ask me why the bosses couldn't have planned that budget-cutting move before I spent every last dime I had hauling myself across the country, but that's how it happened. Less than two weeks into my television career, I was fired.

It was devastating and humiliating. There I was, sitting cross-legged on my bed in that tiny apartment with the clanging radiator, crying over the career that ended before it ever started. *I will laugh about this someday,* I remember telling myself. *But that day is not today.* I felt like I had hit bottom. (And if memory serves, I did hit the bottom of many pints.) I had nowhere to go but back home, back to my childhood bedroom, back to the friends who had just sent me off with such hope only weeks before. Failure to launch. I drove the two-day trek back home through Idaho and Utah and Arizona, all alone with my thoughts. I felt sorry for myself. I wondered if I should just toss this crazy dream aside and get a normal job in PR like so many of my friends had done.

But after licking my wounds for a few weeks, I decided to stay on the path. I started my job search again. Square one: sending out résumé reels around the country, trying to land that first big break—again. Sure enough, within just a month or so, I did. And here's the thing—this time, it was a better job. Much better. A bigger market, and a bigger newsroom. Even a bigger salary ($15,000!). And it hit me: I wouldn't have gotten that job if I hadn't had the experience, brief as it was, from my ten-day career in Butte, Montana.

Lesson one: there is no such thing as a wasted opportunity—not if you are determined to make something of it. Just keep going.

Lesson two: you've got to leave home.

Not literally, of course. You don't have to embark on your own Tucson-to-Butte pilgrimage. But you might have to leave your emotional home base, your comfort zone, your wheelhouse, the place you feel safe, where you are usually right and rarely challenged. Comfortable is not where the action is. It is not where you will find out who you really are.

To discover your purpose, you probably need to get uncomfortable. I don't know why, but the most fruitful seasons of blossoming and growth are always, always, inevitably, on the other side of risk. On the other side of a bold choice. On the edge, waiting for you, on the other side of your fear.

> Comfortable is not where the action is. It is not where you will find out who you really are.

God is waiting there too.

When we step out of our comfort zones, we step into our need. This is where God gets a chance to do his thing. Yes, he shows us what we're made of, but he shows us what he is made of too. We lean on him, trust him, hope in him—and start to know him in a whole new way.

Let's be clear. This is not a vague assurance that he will work things out just as you wanted. It is a simple certainty that he will be there to catch you. And the jump will be worth it—if only just to learn that.

I have taken a few jumps during my life. Remember that television career we just talked about? The one I toiled so hard to launch? It was going pretty well. I worked for nearly six years in local news, rising from station to bigger station and ending up back in my hometown anchoring the weekend news at the local NBC affiliate. I had a good job and a decent apartment and was surrounded by friends and family.

That's when I decided to blow it up and go to law school (career ruining number two).

I moved across the country to Washington, DC, leaving everything familiar behind again.

Fast-forward. (Do you really want to hear about contracts and statutes and torts?) I graduated from law school at Georgetown.

I passed the bar and worked at a big law firm. I lined up a clerkship with a prestigious federal judge. It was the kind of opportunity that young lawyers clamor for, the kind of move that can make your career, set you on a path to stellar legal success. I was just months away from reporting for duty at the courthouse. My course was set.

And then, I had an epiphany. This wasn't really my dream. It might be someone else's, but it wasn't mine.

All those years, I was embarrassed to admit my ambition to myself. But suddenly, I couldn't deny it. What I really wanted was to go back to my roots in journalism. I still had that nagging dream to really make it in television news—this time on a national level. What I did next was insane and unthinkable. I quit the clerkship before I even started.

(Career ruined tally: three.)

I don't know how much you have heard about these clerkships, but no one ever says no to a federal judge. It does not happen. I went to meet the judge, to break up in person. I will never forget what he asked me. "Do you have a job?" No, I told him. "Do you have any prospects, any leads?" I shook my head. No.

"Okay," he said, baffled at this lunatic in his office, probably wondering what he had ever seen in me in the first place. But he graciously tried to salvage the situation and counsel me. "I understand what you are saying," he said. "But why don't you come work for me for a year? It will only enhance your opportunities, and then you can go chase your dreams."

Just me and him. Sitting on his couch in his austere chambers. Moment of truth.

I looked at him and said, "I know you are right, and everything you say makes perfect sense. But I also know myself, and I know that if I don't do this right now, I will never have the guts again." He sighed, smiled, wished me luck, and walked me to the door. A great human.

It was my moment of truth, my moment to jump.

I walked out of that courthouse and realized I had . . . nothing. Less than nothing. I had blown up my whole perfectly laid out legal future. But I jumped anyway, and long story short, I found a job with a legal network a few months later. It was the heyday of televised trials, and Court TV happened to be looking for a correspondent who was an attorney and had on-air experience. In other words, it was perfect for me. And just like that, my multiple career ruinings became my career path. My vision for myself started to come true.

———

I'm not here to tell you it was easy. There were some wilderness months there. Long nights of tossing, turning, and second-guessing. I didn't know there would be a happy ending. And that's the point.

You have to take a leap a time or two in this life. Sometimes it's your decision; sometimes life nudges you off the edge. You'll jump, and sometimes, you will stick the landing. There you are—both feet planted. Legs strong. Spirits high. Looking back with a huge smile on your face . . . the crowd gathers and stares at you in awe. They wave and applaud; they marvel at your brilliance and grace. You just got ten billion likes on social media.

And other times—more than I care to tell you—you will not stick the landing. You will land wobbly and drop to your knees. Or you will fall, miss the mark by a mile, and descend. Right down to the bottom. You will be banged up, scratched, embarrassed, and a little bloody. And what you do next will determine everything.

You'll climb.

You'll stick with it because you are not climbing alone. God is with you, and he is for you. In fact, he is ready to carry you if you'll let him. Failing and floundering and finding out that God is loyal and true anyway—I can think of no experience that bonds us more strongly to him and strengthens our faith.

I'm back at the podium. I'm in my hot robe and my silly hat clutching my fake degree. Commencing my commencement.

Here it is. My pockets emptied. The things I would like to tell my younger self.

Even our wrong decisions can be redeemed; it's never over. This choice or that choice isn't the definitive end or the only possible beginning. Whatever you did—within reason, of course (and the law)—you didn't irreversibly destroy your life or career. You might just be going a different way.

Or maybe you really did throw yourself way off course, making the trip harder and more winding. This is a great moment for God to shine. Invite him into your chaos. Faith is believing God will take you where you're meant to go, one way or the other. You cannot write yourself out of your destiny. He won't let you.

God can refashion our disasters and failings into something redeeming. The challenges we come across, the cliffs we climb, the weight we carry—this is what makes something of us that is worthy and strong. This is what prepares us for future greatness and our most stunning leaps.

Why does life have to be that way? I don't know, and neither do you. It's just like that. So learn to make friends with your troubles—make them your teachers, instead of your tormentors. Or imagine they're rescuing you, pointing you in a different direction, to what's truly meant for you.

Even our wrong decisions can be redeemed; it's never over.

Here is what I know. Your obstacles, your broken places, the spots where you've healed, the things you've overcome—this is the source of your strength and also the source of your beauty. You will come to a time when you say, "I'm so glad that thing I feared or dreaded happened because I would not be me without it. I wouldn't have learned compassion or empathy. I would not have known the determination or grit deep within me."

Through risk, through adversity, God reveals himself and our true selves. Our purpose, our significance, our meaning. That path, we cannot ruin.

> In their hearts humans plan their course,
> but the LORD establishes their steps.
>
> Proverbs 16:9

CHAPTER 30

COMMUNION

T he body of Christ, broken for you. The blood of Christ, shed for you."

The sacred words of Communion—uttered weekly in churches worldwide, in every language imaginable. The exact phrasing might differ by denomination or tradition, but the ritual is the same, the ceremony inaugurated by Jesus at the Last Supper. I have heard a version of these words hundreds if not thousands of times. Perhaps you have too. But until recently, I had never spoken them.

At my church in New York City, as in most, volunteers are essential. Volunteer greeters, volunteer setup, volunteer takedown, volunteer A/V, volunteer choir, volunteer readers, volunteer organizer of volunteers. Our beloved pastors are the church's leaders, but come Sunday, the members make the place work.

At our services, parishioners even help with Communion. Though I had been attending this church for nearly a decade, pitching in often to write prayers or a benediction (even giving a "sermon" once or twice!), in all of those years I had never volunteered for Communion. Perhaps I was intimidated, perhaps I felt unworthy. Perhaps I preferred to be alone at church, burrowing into my own spiritual silo.

One day, however, I felt moved to ask, "Do you think I could help with Communion someday?" The volunteer coordinator, uber-efficient and ever fending off gaps in the schedule, penciled me right in.

Pastor Michael holds the plate of bread; I hold the cup. We stand at the center of the sanctuary. The music begins. One by one, they come forward.

People. Every kind. Hearts open, ready to receive. They take the wafer. Pastor Michael speaks.

The body of Christ, broken for you.

They dip the host into the cup of wine. I meet their eyes.

The blood of Christ, shed for you.

The ritual repeats. Again, and again. They come, they come, they come. Some confidently and joyfully, some shyly or forlornly.

The blood of Christ, shed for you.

The blood of Christ, shed for you.

The blood of Christ, shed for you.

It is repetition yet feels the opposite of rote. On the contrary, every interaction feels unique unto itself, weighted with significance—God's private moment with every human heart.

What a rare, remarkable privilege to share in giving this blessing, to play this momentary part. As I stand, watching people slowly file forward, I'm struck anew that God's promise of rescue, his great redemption pact with humanity, is personal, specific, addressed to each individual. It belongs to me, to you, and to them. In this, there is no "other."

But most importantly, it belongs to us.

Communion.

The word itself reminds us the sacrament is not meant to be a lonely one, done in isolation. It is, by definition, communal. We encounter God, but we also encounter each other. We do it together because the promise is ours together—a tie that binds us to each other for eternity. Not just for Sunday morning. For everywhere and for always.

It is a profound and moving experience to look our fellow human beings in the eye and for a moment, for just a split second, imagine how God views them—with the eyes of a father upon dearly loved children.

> See what great love the Father has lavished on us, that we should be called children of God! And that is what we are!
>
> 1 John 3:1

God's promise of
rescue, his great
redemption pact with
humanity, is personal,
specific, addressed to
each individual.

And if we are his children, then you and I are also brothers and sisters. Siblings. Family.

Sometimes this feeling of community comes over me far outside the sanctuary walls, as I walk the streets of my neighborhood or ride the subway. For a moment, I find myself pulled up and away from the distraction of my phone or the preoccupations of my inner world. I squint mentally to adjust my gaze, trying to see what God sees.

It is overwhelming. Some people fascinate me, repel me, or downright scare me. This is New York City, after all. But in these moments of reflection—rarer than they should be—I endeavor to move past my fears and shallow assumptions and consider each person individually. I strive to see them through God's eyes, as they truly are, each bearing his image. I contemplate them, remembering that, like me, every human being travels their own path. For some, this could be the greatest day of their life. Perhaps they got engaged or received that big promotion they had been hoping for. Maybe they won the lottery (why are they still riding the subway?)! For others, it could be the worst of times—the discovery of a betrayal, the loss of a job, a devastating diagnosis. For most, it is probably just an average Tuesday. Whatever may be, God intimately knows them all. Their history, their hearts, their hopes and aspirations. Their aches and private agonies.

God knows us down to bone, cell, and marrow—the beloved creations he has "fearfully and wonderfully made" (Psalm 139:14). I can only marvel: the way God knows me, the depths of his care for me, is exactly how he knows each one of them.

Our God is a people person.

Our God is a people person.

Honestly, I don't know how he does it. How does God maintain love to "a thousand generations" (Exodus 34:7 NAB)? Just another unfathomable mystery, another question that can't be answered, another occasion for the exercise of deep faith. He does it because he is God.

It's much harder for us. But that doesn't mean we shouldn't try.

> "A new command I give you. Love one another.
> As I have loved you, so you must love one another."
>
> John 13:34

We are all different. Some of our differences are intriguing and awe-inspiring and delightful. Some are disturbing or alarming. Some offend or terrify us.

Everything in our modern culture seems designed to remind us of our differences and deepen our divide. The pull is irresistible; sometimes, it even feels righteous. Are we supposed to judge others? The Bible says no! ("Do not judge, or you too will be judged" [Matthew 7:1]). And the Bible says yes! ("The person with the Spirit makes judgments about all things" [1 Corinthians 2:15]).

Alas, even this amounts to another point of difference between us.

When I am overwhelmed by these matters, I throw my hands up. Not in resignation but in supplication. I need help. I need discernment. But most of all, I need love. This part is not ambiguous;

it is not up for theological debate. However we approach our fellow humans, we are to do so in love. Whatever our differences.

> **Allow God to be as creative and original with others as he is with you.**[1]
> **Oswald Chambers, *My Utmost for His Highest***

When we are "rooted and established in love" (Ephesians 3:17), we are fortified and better equipped to accept each other's differences with grace. With trust in God's judgment—in his justness and his mercy—and with confidence in his character, we can strive to set aside those feelings of threat, distrust, or dislike, and look upon one another in love.

We will still disagree, sometimes fiercely, and justifiably so. We are human. But our faith calls us to give our fears and concerns and resentments over to God so that what remains is love. He carries the weight of difference so that we can be light.

"Let your light shine before others."

Matthew 5:16

Before we share the bread and cup, Pastor Michael takes a moment to remind us that this sacrament, the Eucharist, means thanksgiving. "Let this be a gesture of your open heart," he says. Then, reading from the ancient liturgy, together we declare our faith:

GREAT IS THE MYSTERY OF FAITH.
CHRIST HAS DIED. CHRIST IS RISEN.
CHRIST WILL COME AGAIN.
THESE ARE GOD'S HOLY GIFTS FOR GOD'S HOLY PEOPLE.

A holy gift. It extends beyond the bread and the wine. The gift is not just Communion but community.

We do this practice together to remind us that we are not alone. We are not meant to be a loosely affiliated assemblage of independents and loners, each to their own. We are to be one, a people vastly different in innumerable ways, yet united by the love we see in God.

> "Do this in remembrance of me."
>
> Luke 22:19

However we approach
our fellow humans, we
are to do so in love.
Whatever our differences.

CHAPTER 31

THE LAST WORD

I once found myself on a long flight listening to *Oprah's Master Class*—a multipart series in which accomplished and inspiring figures tell the stories of their paths to success. Hearing about the journeys of the likes of Maya Angelou or Tyler Perry or John Lewis is often moving and always inspiring. Other people's lives can be incredible teachers.

Oprah told of her against-all-odds journey from a childhood of poverty and abuse in Mississippi to the heights of worldwide influence and icon status. I wasn't listening for broadcasting tips, though I would certainly love to have a coffee with her one day and learn at the feet of the master. (Oprah, call me!)

The lessons she imparted were more soulful than tactical, raising deep and probing questions—vintage Oprah. But on this occasion, she posed a question to herself. After all the struggles, all the success, and all the back-and-forth along the way, she asked herself, *What is my purpose?*

It's a question with penetrating potential.

The question is not *What is my job?* It's not *What are my goals?* Or *What is my identity (mother, wife, daughter, friend, etc.)?* And the answer is not something specific or narrow: *I'm here to build houses for the poor. I'm here to provide for my family. I'm here to raise good humans.* Even if worthy or altruistic, those things are not our purpose. The query is broader, wider, and deeper. *Who am I? What are the qualities God uniquely has given me? What is the best use of those gifts while I am on this planet?*

> Who am I? What are the qualities God uniquely has given me? What is the best use of those gifts while I am on this planet?

Oprah had a good answer (of course). Her purpose—her ultimate reason for being—was "to be a sweet inspiration."[1] It was a deep knowing within her that she recognized even as a little girl the very first time she spoke at church, a calling that carried her and catapulted her.

My first thought upon hearing this was, *Oooh, good one. Can that be my purpose too?* But you can't steal someone else's life purpose, especially not Oprah's.

I know what my purpose isn't. It isn't to be on television or be famous; it isn't even to tell important stories (though I aspire to that purpose at work).

I've known since I was a little girl that I am a communicator and an explainer. I always had a vision of myself standing at the front of a room, gesturing to a blackboard or something, pointing out things. Early on, I thought that meant maybe I was supposed to be a teacher. When I discovered broadcast journalism midway through college, it gelled with that childhood vision. I loved telling people the news; I was drawn to complex subjects—politics, legal cases—I enjoyed the challenge of taking complicated things and boiling it all down to basic terms. Also, I loved just . . . talking. Later I went to law school, and that made sense too. I imagined standing up in court, making an impassioned argument, giving voice to those who needed an advocate.

I like to speak; I like to write. I love the feel of words on my lips or on my fingertips when I type (so much that I have wished all my life I could learn another language—even more words to have at my disposal!). Writing, speaking, persuading, teaching—this is my true north.

Sometimes, though—too many times to count—my tongue has been sharp. Quick, harsh, searing. Clever or funny at the expense of someone else—and the cost ultimately to myself. "Set a guard over my mouth" (Psalm 141:3), the scripture says, and no one needs this prayer more than I. When I was a sassy teenager, my big mouthy mouth used to drive my father crazy. He even started calling me "Last Word" because I kept talking in any argument or conflict. I just couldn't . . . shut . . . up. Even when it was for my own good. Even when I was digging myself deeper. Even when I stopped making sense. Had to get in that last word.

Our purpose is more than what we happen to be good at, for even our gifts can be used in ways that fall short of love. I believe we feel in sync with ourselves and with God when we do what we are uniquely suited to do for something meaningful, in service to something or someone greater than ourselves.

$$\frac{\text{God-Given Talents} + \text{Service to Something Greater}}{\text{Purpose}} =$$

God has given me more than a big mouth. He has given me a voice. He has woven together my life into a surprising tapestry I never could have imagined, far more than I deserve, far beyond what I would ever have hoped for or dared to dream. I am no missionary. Every day I inevitably fall short. But God's mercies are new every morning.

> **May you find a harmony between
> your soul and your life.[2]**
> **John O'Donohue, *To Bless the Space Between Us***

Even now, I'm not sure I know what my purpose is. Maybe it changes over the seasons of life. At this moment, at this writing, here is what I think it is. With humility and trepidation—I'm honestly terrified of what you might think!—I will share it with you.

It boils down to one word. That one, actually. Simple but not easy. Interestingly, it is the word I enter every day in Wordle[3] as my first guess.

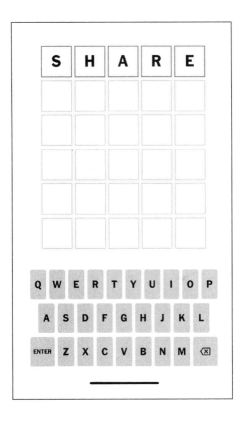

Share.

A good Wordle starter and mantra for life. In one tiny word—a dynamic, multifaceted call to action.

To share what we have been given is an act of faith and trust in God. This does not come naturally to me. I am congenitally fearful, guilty, and worried—ever anxious that I am, at any and all times, mere moments away from calamity, my comeuppance, my good fortune to end, for me to get what I surely deserve. These feelings cannot be from God. If left to fester, they are an affront and vote of no confidence in God. To be fearful of losing what we have been given, to hoard what we have—emotionally, spiritually—is to forget that it is, and has always been, a gift from God. Pure grace. That he who has me will hold me to the last day.

God is "able to do immeasurably more than all we ask or imagine" (Ephesians 3:20). True to his word, he has blessed me beyond comprehension and certainly beyond merit. But I have asked myself, *Why?* Sometimes my comfortable life has made me uncomfortable. Sure, I have endured hardships, as most people have. But my blessings far exceed them. It makes no sense to me. I do not deserve it. I did not earn it. It is not false humility or misplaced modesty to identify God as the source of all the good I have experienced in my life. Why me? There is no reason. The only thing I know, the only sense I can make of it, is that God gave me these blessings not to keep or hoard or store away for a rainy day but to share. To give what I have been given. To tell what I have been told.

> The place God calls you to is the place where your
> deep gladness and the world's deep hunger meet.[4]
> **Frederick Buechner,**
> *Wishful Thinking: A Seeker's ABC*

Mostly what God
does is love you.
If we can believe
this, really believe
this, how different
would we be?

I am here in this moment to share my voice, my heart. To share this truth, this single truth. A truth I need to hear as much as I need to tell. A truth I need to believe as much as I need to share.

Mostly what God does is love you.

If we can believe this, really believe this, how different would we be? How different would our lives be? How different would our world be?

One of the leaders at my church, Kate Gungor, gave a beautiful sermon in which she talked about how a key part of our understanding of God has to do with wonder and awe—that sense of astonishment and reverent surprise when we encounter him. It's the kind of sentiment that can often overcome us when we witness and enjoy the natural world, when our eyes behold beauty: stars and oceans and blooms and mountains and galaxies and high notes and breezes and babies' toes. Kate read a quote from Abraham Joshua Heschel: "Awe is an intuition for the dignity of all things, a realization that things not only are what they are but also stand, however remotely, for something supreme. Awe is a sense for the transcendence, for the reference everywhere to mystery beyond all things."[5]

And then she said: "The paradox of faith is the love of God that creates us to be in awe of God, is also in awe of us. . . . God is taken by you."[6]

There it is again.

Mostly what God does is love us.

May love have the last word.

ACKNOWLEDGMENTS

I really do believe the mantra I so often share with younger people: anything interesting you do in life will be outside your comfort zone. With this book, I was forced to take my own advice. Out on faith and out on a limb, I wouldn't have had the courage to embark on this endeavor without the gentle but insistent, *yearslong* prodding of my literary agent, Cait Hoyt, and the wisdom, inspiration, and ever-clever pep talks of Damon Reiss, who graciously agreed to come out of editor retirement just for me. My gratitude and respect are with Stephanie Newton, Rachel Buller, Meg Schmidt, and the entire team at W Publishing and HarperCollins Christian Publishing. Thank you to Joel Muddamalle, a real-life, honest-to-goodness theologian who graciously lent his expertise to reviewing this manuscript. And if you ever find yourself attempting something hard and scary, I hope you have someone as irrepressibly enthusiastic as Hoda Kotb—and her two giant pom poms—cheering you to the finish line.

There really is nothing new under the sun (Ecclesiastes 1:9) when it comes to writing about faith; all the thoughts and observations here are an amalgam of the many, many spiritual teachers and examples I have loved and admired and learned from along the way—some up close, some from a distance. To name just a few: Charley and Nancy Guthrie, Teri Stauffer, Roger Barrier, Anne Burnson, Tom Copps, Eugene Peterson, Beth Moore, Tim Keller, Mark Batterson, Michael Rudzena, David and Kate Gungor, Bishop Ed Gungor, Father Greg Adolf, and Shauna Niequist.

My husband, Michael Feldman, is my wisest confidant and greatest encourager. This project quite simply wouldn't have happened without him. My children are my reason for being *and* for writing. I hope they read this one day. It is mostly what I'd want them to know about the God that loves them so.

Finally, I am grateful for the deeply feeling and faithful home I grew up in and the people who first loved and shaped me: Mom, Dad, sis, and big brother. And, of course, "the sixth member" of our family, who started a good thing in me and will see it to completion (Philippians 1:6).

NOTES

Introduction

1. Richard P. Feynman, *Six Easy Pieces: Essentials of Physics Explained by Its Most Brilliant Teacher*, 4th ed. (New York: Hachette: Basic Books, 2011).

Chapter 3: The Bonus Commandment

1. *SNL*, "Stuart Smalley—Daily Affirmations," streamed September 16, 2023, *PuckMonkey*, February 22, 2011, YouTube video, 0:47, https://www.youtube.com/watch?v=6ldAQ6Rh5ZI.
2. Dan Burke, "Lectio Divina, A Guide: What It Is & How It Helps Prayer Life," SpiritualDirection.com, April 21, 2012, https://spiritualdirection.com/2012/04/21/what-is-lectio-divina-and-will-it-help-my-prayer-life-a-guide-to-lectio-divina.

Chapter 4: Like a Mother

1. Elizabeth Stone, "Making the Decision to Have a Child Is Momentous," Human Coalition, accessed September 16, 2023, https://www.humancoalition.org/graphics/making-decision-child-momentous/.

Chapter 5: You're Soaking in It

1. John Piper, "Who Is the Disciple Jesus Loved?," *Desiring God*, episode 1642, June 21, 2021, https://www.desiringgod.org/interviews/who-is-the-disciple-jesus-loved.
2. Oswald Chambers, "Inner Invincibility," *My Utmost for His Highest*, accessed September 16, 2023. https://utmost.org/inner-invincibility/.

Chapter 7: God's Telephone Number

1. Susan Braudy, "He's Woody Allen's Not-So-Silent Partner," *New York Times*, Section 2: Arts and Leisure, August 21, 1977, p. 11.

Chapter 8: He Speaks Our Language

1. Drew Weisholtz, "Kristin Chenoweth Reflects on Finding 'God's Grace' After Near-Death Accident on TV Set," *Today*, April 7, 2023, www.today.com/popculture/kristin-chenoweth-reflects-on-faith-rcna78645.
2. Susan Filan to Savannah Guthrie, March 17, 2017.

Chapter 10: Praying When You Can't

1. Beth Moore, *All My Knotted-Up Life: A Memoir* (Carol Stream, IL: Tyndale House, 2023), 14.
2. Shauna Niequist, *I Guess I Haven't Learned That Yet* (Grand Rapids, MI: Zondervan, 2022).
3. Niequist, *I Guess I Haven't Learned That Yet*, 110.

Chapter 11: Psalm 23

1. Henry van Dyke, "Joyful, Joyful, We Adore Thee," Hymnary.org, 1907, accessed September 16, 2023, https://hymnary.org/text /joyful_joyful_we_adore_thee.

2. Eugene Peterson, *Living the Message: Daily Help for Living the God-Centered Life* (San Francisco: HarperOne, 1996), 157–58.

Chapter 12: A Beautiful Day in the Neighborhood

1. Micah Fitzerman-Blue and Noah Harpster, *A Beautiful Day in the Neighborhood*, Script Savant, accessed September 16, 2023, https://the scriptsavant.com/movies/A_Beautiful_Day_In_The_Neighborhood.pdf.

Chapter 13: Garment of Praise

1. "Larry King Show—Joni Eareckson Tada Story," brunetachka, June 6, 2009, https://www.youtube.com/watch?v=Foffh-gneRs.

2. "Larry King Show—Joni Eareckson Tada Story."

Chapter 14: Turn Your Eyes

1. Rick Warren, *The Purpose Driven Life* (Grand Rapids, MI: Zondervan, 2002), 314.

2. Helen Lemmel, "Turn Your Eyes upon Jesus," Hymnary.org, 1922, accessed October 25, 2023, https://hymnary.org/text/o_soul_are _you_weary_and_troubled.

Chapter 16: Believing Is Beautiful (Or, The Shape of Faith)

1. Bruce Wilkinson, *The Prayer of Jabez: Breaking Through to the Blessed Life* (Sisters, OR: Multnomah, 2000), 23.

Chapter 17: Down to the River

1. *The Merchant of Venice*, ed. David Bevington et al. (New York: Bantam Books, 2005), 4.1.182–184.

Chapter 18: Thou Changest Not

1. Thomas O. Chisholm, "Great Is Thy Faithfulness," Hymnary.org, 1923, accessed September 16, 2023, https://hymnary.org/text/great _is_thy_faithfulness_o_god_my_fathe.
2. Chisholm, "Great Is Thy Faithfulness."

Chapter 20: He Reclined

1. Sarah Bessey, "Why I Gave Up Drinking," *Relevant*, August 1, 2022, https://relevantmagazine.com/life5/why-i-gave-up-alcohol/.
2. Bessey, "Why I Gave Up Drinking."
3. Bessey, "Why I Gave Up Drinking."

Chapter 21: Mercy Me

1. *The Mission*, directed by Roland Joffé (1986; Los Angeles: Columbia Pictures, 1986), DVD.
2. *The Mission*.
3. N. T. Wright, *Evil and the Justice of God* (Westmont, IL: InterVarsity Press, 2013), 164–65.

Chapter 22: Jesus Answered

1. "Reason is on our side, love," from "Miracle Drug," track 2 on U2, How to Dismantle an Atomic Bomb, Island Records, 2004, https:// www.u2.com/lyrics/85.

Chapter 23: The Overnight Note

1. N. T. Wright, *Evil and the Justice of God*, 164–65.

Chapter 25: What About Job?

1. Scott Pelley, "Return to Newtown, 4 Years Later," *60 Minutes*, August 6, 2017, https://www.cbsnews.com/news/return-to-newton -ct-sandy-hook-school-shooting-4-years-later-2/.

2. Peter Wehner, "My Friend, Tim Keller," *Atlantic*, May 21, 2023, https://www.theatlantic.com/ideas/archive/2023/05/tim-keller/674128/.

Chapter 26: Send Me Home

1. Peter Wehner, "My Friend, Tim Keller," *Atlantic*, May 21, 2023, https://www.theatlantic.com/ideas/archive/2023/05/tim-keller/674128/.
2. Matt Smethurst, "50 Quotes from Tim Keller (1950–2023)," Gospel Coalition, May 19, 2023, https://www.thegospelcoalition.org/article/50-quotes-tim-keller/.
3. Michael Gryboski, "Tim Keller's Son Says His Dad Is Being Moved to Hospice at Home, Says He's 'Ready to See Jesus,'" *Christian Post*, May 18, 2023, https://www.christianpost.com/news/tim-kellers-son-says-his-dad-is-being-moved-to-hospice-at-home.html.
4. Gryboski, "Tim Keller's Son Says His Dad Is Being Moved to Hospice at Home."

Chapter 27: The Fragrance of the Gospel

1. "You Give Love a Bad Name," track 2 on Bon Jovi, Slippery When Wet, Universal: Mercury, 1986.
2. Glenn Stanton, "FactChecker: Misquoting Francis of Assisi," Gospel Coalition, July 10, 2012, https://www.thegospelcoalition.org/article/factchecker-misquoting-francis-of-assisi/.

Chapter 30: Communion

1. Oswald Chambers, "Getting There," *My Utmost for His Highest*, accessed September 16, 2023, https://utmost.org/getting-there-3/.

Chapter 31: The Last Word

1. Oprah Winfrey, Oprah's Master Class, OWN TV, (c) Harpo, Inc., https://www.oprah.com/app/master-class.html.

2. John O'Donohue, *To Bless the Space Between Us: A Book of Blessings* (New York: Doubleday, 2008), 44.

3. Wordle, New York Times, https://www.nytimes.com/games/wordle/.

4. Frederick Buechner, *Wishful Thinking: A Seeker's ABC* (San Francisco: HarperOne, 1993), 118–19.

5. Abraham Joshua Heschel, *I Asked for Wonder: A Spiritual Anthology*, ed. Samuel H. Dresner (Chestnut Ridge, NY: Crossroad Publishing, 1983), 3.

6. Kate Gungor, "Good Shepherd New York - 6.11.23," Good Shepherd Church, June 11, 2023, YouTube video, 39:53, https://www.youtube.com/watch?v=a66Ugx2U-XQ.

ABOUT THE
AUTHOR

Savannah Guthrie is the coanchor of NBC News' TODAY, NBC News' chief legal correspondent, and a primary anchor for the network's election and special events coverage. A former White House correspondent, she has anchored debates and town halls and conducted a wide range of exclusive and headline-making interviews, from presidents and prime ministers to some of the most recognizable figures in the world. An Emmy, Murrow, and Peabody Award recipient, Savannah was inducted into the Broadcasting and Cable Hall of Fame in 2022. She is a graduate of the University of Arizona and Georgetown Law and a *New York Times* bestselling author of the children's book series *Princesses Wear Pants*. She is the executive producer of the Netflix show *Princess Power*, based on the books.

Savannah has been married to communications consultant Michael Feldman since 2014 and the couple has a daughter, Vale, and a son, Charley. She is as an ambassador for Best Buddies, which serves individuals with intellectual disabilities as well as an ambassador for the Elizabeth Dole Foundation's Hidden Heroes campaign for military caregivers. In her downtime, she enjoys dabbling in tennis, pickleball, piano, and guitar as well as making a dent in her perpetual sleep deficit. She attends Good Shepherd Church in Manhattan.